LOSING THE EMPRESS

LOSING THE
EMPRESS

A *Personal Journey*

THE *EMPRESS OF IRELAND'S* ENDURING SHADOW

DAVID CREIGHTON

DUNDURN PRESS
TORONTO · OXFORD

Editorial Co-ordinator: Anthony Hawke
Editor: Barry Jowett
Design: Jennifer Scott
Printer: Transcontinental

Canadian Cataloguing in Publication Data

Creighton, David
    Losing the Empress: a personal journey

ISBN 1-55002-340-3

1. Empress of Ireland (Steamship). 2. Storstad (Steamship). 3. Shipwrecks — Quebec (Province) — Saint Lawrence River Estuary. I. Title.

G530.E4C73 2000   910'.9163'44   C00-931883-6

1   2   3   4   5   04   03   02   01   00

THE CANADA COUNCIL | LE CONSEIL DES ARTS
FOR THE ARTS | DU CANADA
SINCE 1957 | DEPUIS 1957

ONTARIO ARTS COUNCIL
CONSEIL DES ARTS DE L'ONTARIO

We acknowledge the support of the *Canada Council for the Arts* and the *Ontario Arts Council* for our publishing program. We also acknowledge the financial support of the *Government of Canada* through the *Book Publishing Industry Development Program, The Association for the Export of Canadian Books,* and the *Government of Ontario* through the *Ontario Book Publishers Tax Credit* program.

Printed and bound in Canada.
Printed on recycled paper. ♻

www.dundurn.com

Dundurn Press	Dundurn Press	Dundurn Press
8 Market Street	73 Lime Walk	2250 Military Road
Suite 200	Headington, Oxford,	Tonawanda NY
Toronto, Ontario, Canada	England	U.S.A. 14150
M5E 1M6	OX3 7AD	

TABLE OF CONTENTS

PART FIVE MYSTERIOUS CIRCUMSTANCES

For Fred

We are now oriented to the future, and those of us who have been shaped by the rationalism of the modern world cannot easily understand the old forms of spirituality. We are not unlike Newton, one of the first people in the Western world to be wholly imbued by the scientific spirit, who found it impossible to understand mythology. However hard we try to embrace conventional religion, we have a natural tendency to see truth as factual, historical, and empirical.

Karen Armstrong, *The Battle for God*

PART ONE

PEOPLE LEFT ON THE SHORE

SENTIMENT

I N 1914 MY GRANDPARENTS drowned in the *Empress of Ireland* disaster,
leaving five orphans of whom the youngest was four-year-old
Cyrus Creighton. When he also died later in California, his
siblings had his remains brought all the way to Toronto. Why? For
burial in the British soil of his lineage.

"Our hearts are in Canada," said my father. "This may be
sentimentality but what would the world be without sentiment."

When sentiment is at war with reason, which should come first?
For Herman Melville, the answer was clear: "I stand for the heart. To
the dogs with the head." Having written the ultimate shipwreck
novel, *Moby-Dick,* he deserves notice.

Happenstance once found me in the company of oceanographer
Robert Ballard, who sleuthed the *Titanic's* final resting-place. This
man of science told me that in youth, he locked his grandmother
and himself in a room for all-out argument to make her accept
evolutionary theory. Score one for the head.

With my own evangelistic kinfolk I was more timid — keenly
debating the idea of evolution with my father, but fearing that his
faith might be undermined. For me, the heart won out.

Ballard feels that it is wrong when someone attains truth only to
have it denied. Yet between sentiment and truth, which one is prior?
You need both, says he.

SOUL OF A MACHINE

What was it that was needed, what ingenious combinations of shipbuilding, what transverse bulkheads, what skill, what genius — how much experience in money and trained thinking, what learned contriving, to avert that disaster?

Joseph Conrad, "The Lesson of the Collision"
(re: *Empress of Ireland* sinking)

O N FRIDAY, MAY 29, 1998, driving to Quebec City for a gala dinner, I have a flat tire just shy of my goal. And me in my best suit. A wheel bolt objects to being unscrewed, so I must ease my Colt off the highway to enlist a car dealer's help before continuing on.

Canadian Pacific poster, circa 1927. (Canadian Pacific Limited)

Sweaty from toil, I enter the Château Frontenac's ballroom as festivities begin. Light-hearted Quebeckers at my big round table are amused that *la voiture* became a cropper, just like the *Empress of Ireland!*

A multi-media museum will feature this ship, which sank long ago in the Gulf of St Lawrence, and our Benefit Banquet will help to fund it.

The courses are such as First Class might have enjoyed on the fatal night, exactly 84 years before. Quite the thing to do, ever since James Cameron's *Titanic* became a top-grossing film: in one Halifax restaurant, shipwreck buffs do the First Class menu while an actor circulates in the guise of her doomed captain.

Our $150-a-plate meal evokes the glory days of "Empress" liners once operated by a railway, the Canadian Pacific. Their route was more northerly than the one out of New York, taking in the St Lawrence and thus, a shorter span of the Atlantic.

My new friends ask why I drove all this way. As a grandson, I explain, of two people who were on the *Empress* — David and Bertha Creighton of the Salvation Army. (*Are* on the boat, actually, a hard fact I discreetly omit).

A grandson of David and Bertha Creighton, passengers on the *Empress!* They arrange to have me introduced as such to the gathering. Prolonged applause, and a kind of homage: all night I am flooded with invitations, praise for my *eminence*, business cards to be autographed. Like I'm famous!

Yet in childhood I knew my grandparents only from the Last Photograph, taken with their five children before the voyage. Everyone in my generation remembers that portrait, displayed on our living-room pianos; all asked about those people and were told the tragic story of the *Empress*.

Speeches about the proposed museum go on at length, all in French: "*cet important site patrimonial . . . ces précieux artefacts . . . facile d'accès par la route 132 . . . l'histoire importante et tristement . . . les superbes artefacts. . . .*"

Precious as those *Empress* artifacts may be, many have already been wafted away by the four winds. Her main wheel, for instance, went to a Pennsylvania garage.

Meanwhile our dinner advances only to a small bowl of soup. I undertook the long drive to Quebec City on a whim, no time for a square meal along the way. Now I am reeling with hunger, the strain of using my high-school French, a nameless anxiety, the burden of memory.

Finally I head out into the streets for a mid-banquet snack and some fresh air. Along the way I visit the Basilica for a glimpse of its gold Christ and gold cross, gold Virgin, gold saints, gold tabernacle. This is Notre-Dame-de-Québec, the first parish of New France. Faded grandeur: brackets on the pews, meant to hold names of families proudly occupying them, are now empty.

In 1887 the Salvation Army, intent on evangelizing Quebec, staged a march near the Basilica and met a barrage of rocks. Twenty-one Salvationists were seriously injured: blood of the martyrs.

Catholics and Salvationists shared a conviction that heaven lay beyond this earth — golden saints for one, golden streets for the other. Yet Quebeckers, who saw themselves as the Mystical Body of Christ, long denied *l'Armée du Salut* a foothold in their city.

Time has erased the Battle of the Basilica from memory, this edifice now being known chiefly as backdrop for a multimedia show, *Triumph of Faith*. A sparsely attended mass I once witnessed here was barely completed before camcording visitors took over the church: from mysticism to media-obsession.

A couple of candy bars later I am back in the Château Frontenac. The Basilica's secular counterpart. Its lobby, called the Great Hall, once regularly filled with steamer trunks of those sailing on CPR liners. Supreme among these was the second *Empress of Britain*, on which monarchs and movie stars once sailed.

There is a photo of an uncle, Arthur Creighton, in his Canadian Pacific office before a picture of the *Britain*. Quebec City and the Château Frontenac are seen in the background, a classic angle for views of such liners. Arthur's face is out of focus — symbolizing, I would say, the *Empress of Ireland's* presence in his memory: this man was only 8 when it swept his parents to their death.

A quick walk-through of the hotel takes in the Jacques Cartier Room, shaped like the cabin on that explorer's vessel. The bar gives a sweeping view of the river whose name was given by Cartier, sailing it first on the feast-day of St. Laurent.

Then back to the dinner. Those at my table are from Rimouski, opposite where the *Empress of Ireland* went down. I ask about the St.

Arthur Creighton, in front of the *Empress of Britain* painting.

Lawrence: Is it still thought to be holy, as in Jacques Cartier's day?

"A sacred reever at the *first*," one woman laughs. Now it holds a simpler place in Quebec symbology: "The reever is a source of life."

Our entrée appears at last, as autograph requests continue. A Monsieur Godbout humbly asks me to sign his business card, then comes back later for the same on his menu. One woman, perhaps having taken too much wine, imagines that I myself splashed to safety back in 1914.

What makes an old boat special to these Quebeckers? It brings out their compassion, there is *patrimonie* (with touristic tie-in) as well as that ocean-liner magic: icon of the new. One man talks at length about his voyage on the *QE2*. In the boring jumbo-jet era, we fancy another time of elegance, conviviality, *haute cuisine*.

Our banquet is graced by the lieutenant-governor and many politicos. I ask David Zeni, author of *Forgotten Empress*, what he sees in this fine occasion. Gazing at the ballroom's ornate decor and noting that this is a *Canadian Pacific* hotel, he replies, "Fulfillment of a CPR dream."

You could travel the Pacific on a CPR boat, cross Canada aboard a single CPR train, then step onto a Liverpool-bound CPR *Empress* after a night at the Frontenac. Here was modernity — a foretaste of today's information-field linkages — and also the imperial overreach that led to global war.

It was just before World War I that a Norwegian coal-carrier, the *Storstad*, rammed and sank the *Empress of Ireland* in a fog patch. First Class survivors were brought by ambulance to this very hotel, Zeni notes. And here the Court of Inquiry, presided over by Lord Mersey of *Titanic* fame, delivered its findings.

One of the ships must have altered course in the fog, and Mersey blamed the *Storstad*. Yet Zeni, going over the court transcript, began to see through testimony given by the *Empress's* captain, Henry Kendall: "A turn of phrase, an inflection — suddenly I thought, *He's leaving something out.*"

When Kendall was exonerated, the Norwegian government in deep outrage held an inquiry of its own, and declared Kendall to be at fault. Nobody can say what really happened.

Blame has been placed on the steering. *Empress*-type liners were unusual in having all-underwater rudders — and twice, before May 1914, they were involved in collisions that led to commissions of inquiry. The rudders may not have given enough maneuverability; perhaps it was some flaw as basic as my car's stubborn wheel bolt.

Kendall had been an exemplary British seaman, going to sea at 15 and rising in the ranks. Then in fourteen minutes, the time it took for his ship to go down with 1,102 on board, he went from skipper of the *Empress* to lifeboat commander, pulling aboard as many wretched survivors as he could.

Kendall's portrait in the June 6, 1914 *Illustrated London News* is the best: scowl of command, gold braid and brass buttons, a backward lean in his chair. Written below is a kind of contradiction: THE CAPTAIN OF THE ILL-FATED LINER, WHO WENT DOWN WITH HIS SHIP, BUT WAS SAVED AND TAKEN ABOARD THE COLLIDING VESSEL.

The passenger toll for the *Titanic* was 807; for the *Empress of Ireland*, 840. And the chaos was greater, for she sank ten times more quickly. Yet a higher proportion of crew on that grandiose White Star liner meant a greater death total overall, and the high-society aspect raised wider interest.

Joseph Conrad, who explored themes of lost honour in *Lord Jim* and *Heart of Darkness*, took keen interest in the Quebec City inquiry. "A charge of neglect and indifference in the matter of saving lives is

Captain Henry Kendall.
(*Illustrated London News*, June 6, 1914)

the cruellest blow," he noted. "The resentful sea-gods never do sleep," and "mere mortals condemned to unending vigilance are no match for them."

The dessert finally arrives, fruit within a sturdy little dark-chocolate piano nobody knows how to disassemble politely. (Best way: pick up and gnaw.)

And now a speech in English: Ken Marschall, visual historian for Cameron's *Titanic*, heaps praise on the old liners. "These grand vessels are important, they are time capsules of history," he says. "They belong to everyone, and must not become pillage for quick commercial gain."

Straight talk: the sunken *Empress* has been gravely damaged by salvagers in recent years. "This beautiful 1907 Iron Gothic ship — there must be guidelines for preservation, otherwise we are stealing her from our children."

Marschall ends by quoting Old Rose, the fictional heroine of Cameron's *Titanic*. That vessel on the Atlantic's floor, she insisted, was "not just a great dead hulk but a ship with a soul."

The soul of a machine. William Booth, the Salvation Army's founder, raged against what a machine economy did to human souls, and planned to bring the deserving poor into Canadian farmlands. But it was only with modern machines — steamships, railroads — that they could be transported to this Eden.

Major Creighton served Booth's aims in the Army's immigration branch, crisscrossing the ocean on his far-ranging tasks. And on the *Empress* he perished: live by the machine, die by the machine.

Advanced video technology will be found in the new museum, to be built near the disaster site and to feature a giant-screen spectacle, *The Last Voyage of the Empress of Ireland*. Our *diner-benefice* starts a campaign to raise $900,000 for this project, seemingly inspired by the experimental theatre of Robert Lepage (a Quebec City resident) and Disney World:

> *The public will witness its departure from Quebec City and will share the enjoyable moments of the cruise up until the moment of the tragic collision in the middle of the night. The visitors will be in the middle of various special effects such as robots appearing, elements of the scenery moving, artificial fog, the prow of the* Storstad *piercing the room, 3-D images, as well as an impressive soundtrack and sound system. The set will include lifeboats, the bridge, the telegraph post, and a gangway.*

Ancient ceremony at the Basilica now gives way to multimedia liturgies. And similar enhancements await the liner from which my grandparents, in Salvation Army terminology, were "promoted to glory."

A wild Celtic dance performance, as in *Titanic*, ends our banquet. Moviegoers want to match the screen image with something in real life, and nobody can blame them for this. But to see the *Empress* as I do, in terms of *l'Armée du Salut* — would that spoil the pleasure?

I descend into Quebec City's Lower Town, and over to the Bassin Louise, a north-woods evergreen aroma strong on the wind. Along the Breakwater beyond it I follow rusted rails to a lengthy dockside building, crudely updated. This must have been the luggage-handling area through which a multitude passed from train to liner: efficiencies of the Canadian Pacific.

A deck hand from a laker moored there, the *Everglen*, has heard about the lost liner. "Never really got noticed," he remarks. "A thousand killed on her but so what — then the war, thousands and thousands every week." *Forgotten Empress*: horrific World War I news

Breakwater wharf, Quebec City. (David Creighton)

diminished memories of this ship — except among Salvationists, many of whom still recall the tragedy in detail.

May 28, 1914 comes again to the mind's eye. The *Empress of Ireland*, on a lovely afternoon, is ready to sail once more. Sixteen steel lifeboats line the boat-deck, a Englehart collapsible under each — more than enough for all, as required after the *Titanic* disaster — and ten bulkheads reinforce the interior, one dividing the twinned boiler rooms.

Losing the *Empress*, with ninety-five flawless Atlantic crossings to her credit, seems impossible.

Captain Kendall, although only 39, has amassed a quarter-century of sea experience. Yesterday an emergency drill went perfectly: three minutes to crank each bulkhead door shut, less than one to swing out all the lifeboats. Nobody imagines these tasks being done in total darkness, with the ship heavily listing.

A train pulls up and 170 Salvationists, bound for the Army's Third International Congress in London, cross over to the *Empress*. A stir is caused by the Territorial Staff Band, garbed in Mountie-style stetson hats and scarlet uniforms. Their group photo, taken before Toronto's City Hall, will later be reprinted with Xs to mark those who survive — only nine out of the thirty-nine who sail now.

Here is Captain Edward Dodd, sub-editor of the *War Cry*, writing a despatch shortly to be mailed:

> From the train to the Empress was but a few steps, and the
> transfer of passengers and baggage was so silent and swift that
> one would have thought the party was entirely composed of
> seasoned globe-trotters instead of people many of whom had
> never crossed the Atlantic before.

This is only part of Canada's four-hundred-strong delegation to
the Congress, but it includes the saintly commissioner, David Rees,
now leaning meditatively on a railing.

Commissioner David Rees (right) at the *Empress*'s rail on May 28, 1914.
(George Scott Railton Heritage Centre)

The 717 passengers filling Third Class include recent immigrants
— some settled by my grandfather, perhaps — now revisiting their
homeland. Many have already travelled far: M. Studberg from
Winnipeg, Ethel Philips from Saskatoon, Miss E. Brohen from
Edmonton, Ernie Howarth from Calgary, W.J. Brown from Vancouver.

Salvationists make up the bulk of 253 in Second Class. High-society types are sparse, but among the eighty-seven in First Class is plump Ethel Sabina Grundy Paton, a banker's diamond-loving wife. Here too is big-game hunter Sir Henry Seton-Karr.

David Creighton has written just-in-case letters to two brothers, and when safely aboard will compose another to his family, that ends: "Our very best affection & love to all."

A bugle call, and warnings from the stewards: "All aboard that's going ashore!" Smoke pours from the two yellow-and-black funnels.

"O Canada" and "Auld Lang Syne" are rendered by the Staff Band, assembled on the promenade deck. And at 4:27 as ropes are cast off from the bollards, it plays a farewell hymn, deeply prophetic:

God be with you till we meet again!
Keep love's banner floating o'er you;
Smite death's threatening wave before you;
God be with you till we meet again!

Inhaling evergreen fragrance in the dark, I trace a final path those voyagers might have taken. The bollards are empty now, the ship has left.

Black waters lie beyond. Lost ancestors, vanished glories weigh on the mind.

A cabbie beeps his horn at me: someone in a good suit wandering around, maybe with designs on ending it all. He asks if I need a ride. Not now, I reply, just going over a few memories.

THE ARMY'S CARD

OR YEARS I DREW A mental blank whenever the *Empress of Ireland* sinking was mentioned. All very solemn. David Creighton the Salvation Army officer: too bad, but he's gone and I'm alive now.

Everything changed when my Aunt Edith died in 1988. In all the years of her old age I never paid a visit and then, at 93, she was no more. The last of the five *Empress* orphans.

Belatedly I wrote a clan history. The *Empress* disaster was at the centre of all, I found. I became absorbed in its meanings.

One night I went back to the Army citadel attended by my family — East Toronto corps at 107 Cedarvale Avenue. A block away at the Danforth-and-Woodbine corner, there would be open-air meetings at which our band stirringly played songs of redemption. Then bystanders were invited to follow it back to the citadel, join in our fellowship: such was the expectation.

Public exposure of this kind calls for a strong faith. And those entering Army work will keep that faith by journeying from such congenial corps as East Toronto into tiny missions in far-off territories. That night someone was leaving for Africa to do the work — and of course, we sang, "God Be With You Till We Meet Again."

Of all the old memories I felt then, one stood out. Salvationist children had to attend the hall three times each Sunday — two services, plus Sunday school in mid-afternoon — and I had a friend, Ken McGillivray, who endured the same routine.

One night, edgy perhaps from go-to-meeting fatigue, we had a big fistfight outside the citadel as its soldiers, newly filled with the message of love, were leaving. My nose bleeds easily, and I was a mess as the adults moved in to break up our bout. I remember their expressions of intense reproach and alarm.

Much later, I realized that Ken's grandfather and mine had been numbers one and two in the Salvation Army's Immigration Department: mine drowned and his did not.

Settlers were educated by the Army's officers, escorted to their final destinations — many of them on *Empress* liners — and given special cards. What these stated was the very essence of Salvationist care and hope. Here is what the Army's card said:

> *God carry you safely to your new home. Fearlessly calculate upon hard work. Bravely meet new difficulties. Do your duty by your families. Help your comrades. Make Canada a home that will be a credit to the old land. Put God first. Stand by the Army. Save your souls. Meet me in heaven!*

IN FEAR FOR YOUR LIFE

I N 1988, WRITING THE family history, I visited Mount Pleasant Cemetery with a nephew, Paul Creighton. Having also broken ties with Salvationism, painfully, he sees the world much as I do.

The *Empress of Ireland* memorial, to the right off Yonge in Section R, gives an effect of disaster with carved ocean waves, and a seagull flying above a cliff representing the Rock of Ages. Gideon Miller, who tended Army dead in Quebec, conceived an image later carved in Vermont red marble by sculptor Emanuel Hahn.

Empress Memorial. (George Scott Railton Heritage Centre)

"This was a Mayflower sort of thing," Paul reflected: "people left on the shore." Bereaved Salvationists disdain mourning dress in the belief that death means victory; a cross is therefore surmounted by a crown. "The saved people become kings in heaven," he added.

Survivors at Mount Pleasant Cemetery memorial service, May 1961.
(George Scott Railton Heritage Centre)

On every Sunday nearest May 29, Salvationists held a service here to honour the apotheosized *Empress* dead. The youngest survivor, known at first as "flaxen-haired little Gracie Hanagan." was long chosen to place the wreath. Photos of survivors, names handwritten in white over their dark apparel, were taken year by year until none were left.

PROMOTED TO GLORY: the military lingo of a bygone age. War being so evil, why bring that into religion?

Because Christianity *starts* with evil. "Any of us could fail in some manner," said Paul. "There's always disappointment in people, because expectations are so high." The human race has fallen, we must work to raise it.

Redemptiveness lives on among Creightons in secular forms — medicine, education, and, for Paul, structure-restoration work on older buildings. "Salvation!" he laughed.

We went on to the grave of three Creightons, across Mount Pleasant Road in the east side of Section O. Wilfred, the oldest orphan. Cyrus, the youngest. And Will: my father, Paul's grandfather.

Cyrus being unknown to Paul, I explained how he died suddenly in California at 16. How the siblings pooled resources to pay his large medical bills, and the cost of transporting his coffin for burial here. How *Empress* hero Gideon Miller conducted the rites.

The reason for bringing the body here is given in a letter by Will, also then living in California — an explanation that cuts to the marrow:

> *Cyrus was always a Britisher at heart and in fact all of us here, though we be on foreign soil, yet our hearts are in Canada and therefore we do not altogether feel at home or settled. This may be sentimentality but what would the world be without sentiment.*

Before dying, the boy stated a wish to become an Army officer, if only he might be spared. The scene was vividly described by his foster-mother Lottie, a sister-in-law to David Creighton. Cyrus's words of commitment "dispelled the darkness, and enabled us to rejoice in the midst of our sorrow," she said. "What could worldly pleasure or honour, or money do at such times? Nothing! Nothing! NOTHING!"

Preach the Gospel, forswear worldly goods: Paul and I well know this message. To deliver it, Salvationists must invade others' lives. "They're driven by a genuine love," says Paul. "They're in fear for your life."

On May 25, 1989 I was invited by the Salvation Army's Historical Society to a meeting about the *Empress*: "Mr. Michael Soegtrop, a diver, will deliver an illustrated talk. Refreshments and fellowship to follow."

At the George Railton Heritage Centre, on Bayview, I received a warm welcome as always at such Army functions. The centre's display of *Empress* artifacts held enigmas I had never sensed before.

When Lieutenant Alf Keith came aboard the *Storstad*, numb with cold, someone wrapped him in a tablecloth from the captain's cabin. And here was that very item. Keith later identified the main cause of death: "It was the cold that fixed us; that water was like ice."

Here also was a gold-plated cornet used in performances by the 1914 Staff Band, formed largely of officers at the Army headquarters. It belonged to Matthew McGrath, the Staff Band's principal cornetist. He perished and yet the instrument survived, having been sent ahead of him.

The Staff Band's loss was so tragic that the question of its revival became a delicate one. Here on display, nonetheless, was a photo showing "The Ensemble" — a partial reconstruction of the Staff Band including survivors, as seen in 1917.

Keith was in the top row near Bert Greenaway, who had been

Reorganized Staff Band, 1917.
(George Scott Railton Heritage Centre)

able to pull him to safety over the *Storstad's* railing. At lower left sat Greenaway's brother, Tom, who sailed the *Empress* with his bride on their honeymoon; both survived. Ernest Green, shown in the middle row, was not so fortunate: the disaster claimed his sister and both parents.

Ernest's father, Adjutant Harry Green, played comical piano tunes of his own composition as the *Empress's* last journey commenced. When a hymn sing-along followed, Bert asked him to play *There is a Sweet Rest in Heaven* for the newlyweds. As it turned out, not they but the adjutant shortly went to an eternal rest.

Ernest served as an Army officer, ultimately becoming head of the correctional department. Bert also chose officership, resigning only to become Dominion Field Commissioner for the Canadian Boy Scouts. Herbert Wood, at lower right, was not an *Empress* survivor and yet went on to write a vivid account of the sinking, *Till We Meet Again*.

The photo also showed David Creighton's oldest son, Wilfred, with a D wrongly substituted for his first name. Twenty years old when he and four siblings fell under the *Empress's* shadow, Wilfred held close to Salvationism. Looking at this picture, I saw how survivors and the bereaved could hold true to tradition through mutual support.

Another photo portrayed Grace Hanagan with her father, the Staff Band's leader, and his wife. For the next eighty years Grace would often repeat her story, but most awesome was the version told at first:

> *Mama woke me up and dressed me and papa and us went upstairs. There was water coming in all over, and the boat was all slanty, so we couldn't hardly walk. Then all at once the boat was covered with water and went right from under my feet. I went under the water and then I found a piece of board and cried.*

Bandmaster Edward
Hanagan, wife Edith,
daughter Grace.
(George Scott Railton
Heritage Centre)

Here was one of the sashes, white with the crimson crowns, used at the 1914 Congress in London to drape empty chairs where Canadian delegates would have sat. It was given to Frank Morris and passed along "in remembrance of the Loved One who was called to the Heavenly Mansions": his brother Arthur.

For a Swedish officer, Amanda Sandberg, the sashes gave rise to a vision of saved multitudes, dressed as if for marriage, travelling far to heavenly consummation:

They're coming from stormy seas,
They're coming from thorny roads,
They're coming from hills,
They're coming from dales,
They're coming, O God, to Thee.

Here was the postcard mailed at Rimouski by *War Cry* artist Teddy Gray: a self-portrait surrounded by signatures given on the *Empress*. Of those whose names may be read, thirty-three were drowned and fourteen saved.

Postcard sent by *War Cry* artist Teddy Gray.
(George Scott Railton Heritage Centre)

The final glimpse of Gray was by Bandsman William Measures, who occupied the same cabin: "The last I saw of poor Gray he was sitting up in his bunk rubbing the sleep out of his eyes. He is gone, poor fellow."

Brisk Army music started our meeting off. "With steady pace the pilgrim moves / Toward the blissful shore," we sang, hand-clapping the chorus: "'Tis better on before."

'Tis better on before: that abiding theme of good hope. Next was "Land Beyond the Blue" with its vision of "hallelujah heaven": mansions bright, harps, spotless robes, living fountains, golden streets.

Still at meetings such imagery is repeated, as the Army keeps largely to its traditions. And struggles to keep pace with other denominations: in 1914 there were some 100,000 soldiers and now, amid a quadupled population, this total remains the same.

Michael Soegtrop's talk began and I was swept away by his *Empress* experience. He knew the personalities: Captain Kendall ("never the same again"), coal stoker Frank "Lucks" Tower (said to have survived the *Titanic*, then the *Empress* — and the torpedoed *Lusitania* as well). It was because so few millionaires were on the *Empress*, he theorized, that the press gave the disaster such minimal coverage.

The liner's very location was long forgotten, scuba divers rediscovering her only on July 17, 1964. An eccentric Montreal accountant, Philippe Beaudry, then became fascinated by the wreck and made it known. "Come and dive the *Empress*," he said to Soegtrop and many others.

The Quebecois phrase *au bout* — to the limit and then some — has been applied to Beaudry's well-publicized dives. With three men living in my own community, Burlington, he founded an *Empress of Ireland* Historical Society.

This wreck now demonstrates, said Soegtrop, the infirmity of "humanity's most stalwart technology" in the face of nature. Man himself is a tiny land animal, on such dives saved from hypothermic death only by his drysuit's quarter-inch of neoprene.

Soegtrop had a gift for metaphor. Diving the *Empress* for the first time, he was "like a timid schoolboy about to enter a cathedral." Beaudry guided him, the two pulling themselves down on a rope, with three stops to forestall decompression sickness, known as "the bends." An emergency once sent Beaudry to the surface without time to decompress, and the bends paralyzed both arms for two days.

Down they went, an underworld-descent myth come true, toward a multitude of cat's-eye shrimp now affixed to the *Empress* — thus turning her, Soegtrop remarked, into "a big furry sea monster straight out of a low-budget B movie."

I had long visualized the boat in terms of the Army's death-euphemism, "promoted to glory." Her victims entering the celestial beyond, breathing Earth's air no more, apotheosized.

Now I was forced to see it as *a big furry sea monster*. The ship was actually there in space and time, a dream-image no longer.

Soegstrom's slides showed the crow's nest from which the *Storstad* had been sighted. A decomposing lifeboat, still in its davits. A broken skylight over the music room. And a grand piano resting there now, upside down. To Soegtrop, always it seemed as though "somebody is going to look over your shoulder."

I was stung by an atavistic dread: my ancestors' earthly forms are free, roaming the deep waters.

"This is a submerged tomb for eight hundred bodies," said the diver. "There is something that draws me to it; the whole history — it draws me back."

The same dark fascination now claimed me.

LOSING THE *EMPRESS*

FOR ME THE SALVATION Army came to mean band music, lively times, transcontinental friendships, moral probity, laughter, warmth — and the question "Are you saved?"

From onward-Christian-soldier activism I drew apart, for better or worse. And that sunken-ship obligation to persons unknown — I had to forget the *Empress*, as well.

At 14 during a violent thunderstorm I was alone in a pup-tent, thinking. If the next bolt scored a direct hit, would I suddenly be upon golden streets — or worse luck, in the darkness of hell? No. Impossible. Some are able to visualize an afterlife, I cannot.

And one day in the car, I overheard my father and his brother Wilfred pondering the question of immortality. Salvationists raising the *question* of immortality, like any other question on some curious topic like Marilyn Monroe, or seashells: amazing.

"I leave eternity to Thee," says Father Mapple in *Moby-Dick*; "for what is man that he should live out the lifetime of his God?"

I attended Toronto's Victoria College where the far-famed Northrop Frye, having discarded a Fundamentalist "smelly garment" (in his phrase), systematized the larger myths. His own lit-crit attire in turn being cast off, naturally, by newer generations.

In 1967 I wrote a mythology book which displeased my father by linking aboriginal beliefs with Christian ones: that cut to the grain. By this time I also had children, and he would send letters inquiring about Jesus's role in their upbringing. After one of them, I recorded an apt dream:

> I was asked to help someone (farmer?) unearth his mother's urn. In the process he found one case containing the well-preserved faces and torsos of three ancestors side by side. Loins and legs not there. They had old-fashioned moustaches. These were under large limestone (?) blocks. He praised these people and said how it consoled him to have them well-preserved.

"Drive your cart and your plow over the bones of the dead," wrote William Blake in *The Marriage of Heaven and Hell*. I had to find my own life. I had to bury the dead. I had to lose the *Empress*.

THE RIVER

She seemed to swim in oil, so smooth the sea
And quiet on the bridge: the great machine
Called for laconic speech, close-fitting, clean
And whittled to the ship's economy.

E.J. Pratt, "The Titanic"

O N AUTOROUTE 20, PARALLELING the St. Lawrence, I trace the final voyage of the *Empress of Ireland*. It is 1999, late March, two months earlier in the year than when she steamed along the river. So the bordering fields remain snowladen, and overcast skies lend a dreamlike clarity to the long corridor: black against the white, straight and immutable.

Canadian Pacific poster,
circa 1930s.
(Canadian Pacific poster
collection)

The sacred river, named on St. Laurent's feast day. Pious Quebeckers likened it also to the Jordan, where Jesus was baptised by St. John. A *Via Dolorosa* is marked out through Jerusalem's laneways, and Salvationist lore enshrines another here on the St. Lawrence.

La Pocatière: the *Empress*, having cast anchor at 4:27 p.m., would have been five hours into the journey at this point. A spring evening, her lights then coming on. The Congress delegates in Second Class would have finished dining on CPR china around 8:30.

"On the wide sweep of the upper deck was gathered the jolliest party of all," said the *Globe*. In an impromptu concert organized by Salvationists, "songs were sung, jokes told, tricks performed and stories related: music and song, the rattle of applause, the ripple of laughter and the buzz of conversation were wafted over the silent deep."

A male group sang, as reported by Major George Attwell: "The clear voices of those nondrinking, nonsmoking young men — in four-part harmony — rose with clarity into the still air."

Light-hearted Ensign Oliver Mardell, leading choruses of "Rocked in the Cradle of the Deep," would make everyone dip down at the word "deep." A game organized by Captain Rufus Spooner — beloved by my parents for his Cockney high spirits — called for one man to let himself fall over while others, gathered around in a circle, would hasten to keep him upright: this was called "Dead Man."

The *Illustrated London News* later ran a picture epitomizing "joy on a ship of tragic memory": the music room, where a gowned violinist was accompanied at the grand piano. An orchestra at the central well, which played Gounod's "Funeral March of a Marionette" at dinner, put down its instruments at nine.

Music room, *Empress of Ireland*.
(*Illustrated London News*,
June 6, 1914)

My parallel journey shortly bypasses Rivière-du-Loup: 10 p.m. their time. Perhaps by then, David was writing the last letter his family would receive: *Bless you & Edith & Willie & Arthur & Cyrus & give us in due time the pleasure of meeting again with good news and all well. . .*

At Bic, No. 20 veers close to the ice-edged St. Lawrence. A Bach partita plays on the car radio.

David had one more letter to write, a humorous one to friends at the Army's Toronto headquarters down by City Hall. "To the True and Faithful Remaining," he began — ones that didn't get to go.

"The party, after a strenuous day of toil and excitement, are asleep, having partaken rather more sumptuously than is the accustomed habit of members of the Festive Board." Those at headquarters would take lunch together in groups that became comically labelled — the "Board of Directors" comprising higher-ups, for instance. David sat with those who named themselves the "Festive Board": more jokes, more fun.

So David implies that after the modest fare such as the Festive Board consumed at headquarters, those on the *Empress* had received much better, had overindulged, and were now sleeping it off.

Rimouski: where the Gulf begins to open. Dramatic late-afternoon cloudscapes now gather. In ocean-liner days, this was the last place at which letters could be mailed within Canada — and conversely, the first point to receive Old Country news from newly arrived ships.

David added a final paragraph, repeating the phrase he heard at that moment — "Last call for mail!" — and ended with a remembrance of the affable Gideon Miller, well-known to the Festive Board:

So here goes for good success all round. Gideon smiled most graciously at us from the wharf at Quebec. He was an outstanding and striking figure.

Fraternally,
Dave

So here at 1:30 a.m. on May 29, the *Empress* had her last exchange of mail.

The *Musée de la Mer* lies beyond Rimouski on a peninsula jutting into the river — *Pointe au Père*, Father Point — beside a lighthouse once painted by Lawren Harris.

Braving snowdrifts and intense winds, I enter the old wooden structure housing the archives. From two young people working here comes a cordial welcome and more — the phone number of David Saint-Pierre, a local man deeply knowledgeable about the *Empress*.

Many tales are told of the *Titanic*, and the *Empress of Ireland* has a melodramatic one about Henry Kendall. During his previous captaincy of the liner *Montrose*, in 1910, he began to be suspicious about a passenger couple, "Mister and Master Robinson." In the *Daily Mail* he had seen photos of the notorious Dr. Hawley Crippen, who butchered his wife: could this be the villain, fleeing with his mistress disguised as a boy?

Kendall alerted Scotland Yard by telegraph, a detective sailed for Canada by a faster boat, and at Father Point on the St. Lawrence the couple was detained. "You will suffer for this treachery, sir," said the wife-killer, setting his gaze on Kendall. This became known as Crippen's Curse.

Globe headlines, August 1, 1910.

The *Globe*'s Crippen story shared the front page with one on Premier Wilfrid Laurier's "vision of Canada's destiny." Intensive rail construction and *the marvel of wireless* showed Canada embracing technological change, just as we do today in a nation fixed upon the internet.

Kendall, guiding the *Empress* toward Father Point at 1:15 a.m. on May 29, 1914, abruptly remembered the Curse. A ghostly fog gathered as if on cue. The *Empress* continued on — waters calm, skies clear — into that sudden mist.

Further along at Ste. Luce-sur-la-Mer, I look almost directly out to the scene of disaster. A marker by the church gives an account of *la tragedie*.

At 1:38 a.m., lookout Jock Carroll spied the *Storstad* and rang his brass bell: "Ship's masthead spotted on the starboard bow."

Montreal-bound colliers laden with Cape Breton coal often plied the St. Lawrence — Dominion Coal alone operated fourteen of them, including the *Storstad* — and all was routine. Something like tractor-trailors on a superhighway now.

Kendall readily judged that this one would pass to the right. At 1:41 he turned the vessel somewhat to the right, also as usual, setting a course that would have held for the rest of his river passage: north 73 east.

On the collier, then hugging the near coast, First Mate Alfred Toftenes somehow got the idea that the liner had veered sufficiently to pass on the *left*. Therefore a turn to the right was necessary for the *Storstad* — or so it seemed.

James Croall concludes *Fourteen Minutes* with two explanations for error aboard the *Storstad*. Long and narrow ships like the *Empress* being not easily steered, perhaps she swung too far to the right while setting her new course, and the port sidelight, red, appeared just before fog set in. Alternatively, the liner might have been so brightly lit as to render both sidelights indistinct.

Ships that pass in the night; or are drawn into a fatal embrace by error or chance or fate or cause-and-effect or divine will.

The fog descended at 1:45. Toftenes, told by Captain Andersen to call him in such conditions, now did so and was joined by him on the bridge. But the fatal turn had already been made. At this moment, 1:55 a.m., the *Empress* loomed ahead, broadside.

The *Storstad* had a sharp prow reinforced to cut through ice, and 11,500 tons of coal filled her hold. Andersen ordered full astern but at once, the collier ploughed into the *Empress's* starboard side.

Kendall knew instantly that the *Storstad's* prow must remain corklike in the gash to prevent a fatal intake of water. "Keep going ahead!" he shouted through a megaphone to her captain. It was no use: the invading ship twisted backwards and fell away.

Kendall then pushed the engine-order telegraph to *CLOSE WATERTIGHT DOORS*. But as water poured in at a rate of 60,000 gallons per second, this proved impossible.

The ship was doomed. Knowing that she must be beached at once, he telephoned the engine room: "Give me all you can."

"The steam is gone," came the reply. The collier had impacted just astern of the bulkhead separating the boiler rooms, causing a Niagara of water to flood the furnaces. Steam generation halted, the engines died.

So now, within minutes of the collision, Kendall sounded the distress siren to announce, "Prepare to abandon ship." By 2:01, basic power on the *Empress* had been lost. At 2:09 she rolled over, and sank one minute later.

It was catastrophe by chance. And among the victims were those visionary Salvationists.

As the light fades I find another marker, close to the ice-heaped shoreline. *"La plus grande catastrophe maritime au Canada,"* it states. A drawing shows the angle of collision.

Marker, Ste. Luce-sur-la-Mer.
(David Creighton)

Captain Andersen initially feared that his vessel would be the one to go down. Later, a half mile away in the fog, he heard the cries of those who had been flung from the sinking *Empress*: "At first I didn't know what it was; it was like one long, moaning sound."

Henry Kendall was thrown overboard as the *Empress's* twin funnels hit the water. Soon picked up by a lifeboat and taken to the *Storstad*, he unloaded fifty survivors and returned with a few volunteers to gather more. But nearly everyone afloat was now dead.

Returning to the *Storstad*, he rushed to the bridge and confronted Andersen: "You have sunk my ship! You were going full speed in the fog!"

"I was not going full speed," Andersen replied. "*You* were going full speed." A river pilot stepped between to constrain the skippers of boats whose chance collision killed 1,012 people. Some were dying even as the two men wrangled.

Andersen's wife later told of Kendall lying face down, still in his dripping uniform, as he cried, "Why didn't they let me drown? Why didn't they let me drown?"

Kendall might have been referring to his rescuers or, in terms by which Joseph Conrad described the *Empress* disaster, to the sea-gods who never sleep:

> *We have been accustoming ourselves to put our trust in material, technical skill, invention, and scientific contrivances to such an extent that we have come at last to believe that with these things we can overcome the immortal gods themselves.*

For dinner I go to the Versailles Restaurant, an older place with *entrées* not quite up to *Louis-Quatorze* criteria. From here I phone David Saint-Pierre at six, as advised.

"Could you come over to *le musée?*" he asks. "I have a key." We meet in darkness, the gale more brutal than before.

David's interest in the *Empress* arose after reading about Robert Ballard's discovery of the *Titanic*: "Here I was living in Rimouski, aware about this shipwreck and yet understanding so little." Soon he conceived the quest of his life, to reconstruct the last fourteen minutes endured by the *Empress* before sinking, in exact sequence. Everything is to be discovered; almost every day he finds new information.

As a summertime guide, David is always excited to receive visitors here. Many, drawn by the picturesque lighthouse, enter to find out for the first time about the wreck. "I love the story of the *Empress* — the boat, the captain, the people. Poignant."

Artifacts are gathered here in abundance. On an *Empress* lifebelt David traces the letters E, M, P and a few marks remaining from the word "Ireland."

"A lot of things are odd about the *Empress*," he remarks. Who actually handled the wheel at the moment of collision? Why were the CPR records destroyed? Why did Kendall go down to a desk job? "Perhaps he didn't *want* to get on another ship."

Henry Kendall sailed as an apprentice at 15 aboard a square rigger, Australia-bound with a burden of railroad steel, and later became Fourth Officer on a steamer plying the North Atlantic route — which troubled him, as indicated in his memoir *Adventures on the High Seas*: "the formidable fogs of Newfoundland made me seriously consider whether I had chosen rightly."

Ocean struggles instilled in Kendall a stoic creed expressed in Rudyard Kipling's "If"; he enjoined his son both to memorize and to live by this poem, embarrassingly earnest to current taste:

If you can keep your head when all about you
  Are losing theirs and blaming it on you,
If you can trust yourself when all men doubt you,
  But make allowance for their doubting too . . .

One wall is filled with a photo showing the bridge of the *Empress* and her navigators, enlarged to life size. The sextants they employ are matched by a real one from the ship, fastened in place.

Here is a wooden wheel, one of two that Kendall handled on that night. David explains the complex mechanisms by which commands were communicated to the rudder so far away.

David, a descendant of navigators, feels special empathy for Captain Kendall: "It is too big to say that he felt guilty — but by the letters he wrote, it looks like it," he says, quietly adding, "It is not usual for a captain to survive his ship."

The bow of the *Storstad* was merely pushed in — "it was like a *Volvo*, it could absorb the shock" — while the *Empress* was struck at precisely her most vulnerable point: "just there, like an empty box." Once before Kendall had experienced such a collision, during which the ramming ship remained snug in the cavity to prevent much water from entering. "This time, the other captain could *not* stay in."

Moment of collision, 1:56 a.m.
(*Weekend Magazine*, No. 21, 1964)

I have a chance to clear up several mysteries. How could Frank "Lucks" Tower, a coal stoker labouring in a vessel's lowest depths, have escaped as water churned at his feet — and not only from this liner but also the *Titanic* and *Lusitania*? (That is, if we can believe Tower — whose name has not been found on any roster of the *Titanic*'s crew.)

Readily explained:stokers, requiring easy relief from the fierce heat and toil, had special ladders that they would frequently climb to reach the deck.

Was human error to blame, as in the *Challenger* spacecraft fiasco? Carelessness caused that mishap but not this, David affirms. Commanders of the *Empress* and the *Storstad* both saw the danger clearly. "They did the best they could," he says, insisting that both did everything possible to avoid collision: "They were too *much* careful."

E.J. Pratt wrote a long poem, "The Titanic," which depicts the smooth efficiency and the clipped language of command on such liners. He ties the notion of unsinkability to technology's swift advance, notably in wireless communication. This easily bred overconfidence:

And this belief had reached its climax when,
Through wireless waves as yet unstaled by use,
The wonder of the ether had begun

To fold the heavens up and reinduce
That ancient hubris *in the hearts of men* . . .

I am shown the wireless from which the SOS was transmitted. "Main power out in three minutes, battery power gone in another five," David recounts. All was up-to-date for that time, in accordance with lessons newly learned from the *Titanic* disaster. "Even with all of that, it was no use," he observes. "Everything adds up."

Young Ronald Ferguson, in pyjamas, used this very transmitter to type out his 1:56 a.m. message in Morse code — slowly, to make sure the import would be grasped: "Stand by for distress signal. We have hit something."

Already Ferguson was struggling against the steep list. But from Father Point came the instant reply: "OK. Here we are."

Ferguson had enough time to add, "SOS, we have hit something, sinking fast, send help." Asked to give the liner's location, he inaccurately replied, "Twenty minutes past Rimouski," then luckily was able to reach the water. He made it to the *Storstad*.

As an old man, invited back to Rimouski in 1980 by the local newspaper, Ferguson told a story never recorded before. The water's impact had stripped him bare, and Captain Andersen's wife offered her scarf to cover his loins. He thanked her, then unthinkingly tied it around his *neck;* the scarf was still in his possession.

An egg boiler: tiny numbers on a metal bar, ensuring times gauged to close fractions in that pre-electronic era. The 1914 world of quaint mechanisms functioning to make sure all went well — and just then, in Europe, bad diplomacy was ensuring that the first industrialized war would soon be fought.

And now another battle is fought over the *Empress*, between preservationists and salvagers. "She doesn't look like a ship anymore," David reflects: structural ruin will result in the vessel's disappearance, unless this work is halted for good.

He espouses Ballard's view of the *Empress*: she belonged on the ocean surface, and now on the bottom. Not a sentimental matter, but one of deep importance for the future. Ballard spoke of Tutankhamen's tomb, stripped of relics because it was thought that nobody would go to see them in the Valley of the Tombs. The same with the *Empress*: in a few years, many will regret that it is empty.

I ask about the divers. "They just don't get along, I think, all that competition — some act as though this is their wreck, just for having taken more artifacts." He has heard of divers cutting guidelines, to prevent others from reaching some new windfall. "Not many people know about this — it is sad to see."

Nonetheless, respect is due to those who have ventured far into the ship. Some have reached the engine room, now treacherous with wires and pipes. He shows the photo of a woman who perished mysteriously on a dive in 1997: "She got tired, I think."

One shelf holds items of dinner china from the *Empress*. With the complicated border — Second Class. With the flowers — First Class.

A soup tureen and a tea plate in Second Class decoration: my grandparents' world. I am invited to pick up the tureen. Inevitably the question comes to mind: could this very one have been used by them at that final dinner?

Many visitors regard artifact preservation as grave robbery, says David — a moral judgment that I reject, as does he: "We want to be in the presence of these people." Some who condemn artifact-retrieval are seen later, he notes, "with tears in their eyes." These humble items direct the mind toward what it all means, toward the truth of shipwreck and loss.

The basement holds a deck chair from the *Empress*, used locally for many years and now being repainted in the original hues for display. There were two hundred in all, and now we have only this. "Somebody told me about seeing three of them at an antiques store a while back," says David. "Fifteen dollars each — I would have bought every one."

We end up at the archives, where David unrolls a set of detailed plans showing every part of the *Empress*. He points out where she was struck by the *Storstad*. He shows a photo of her at the Breakwater, the Château Frontenac looming beyond.

Now the big question: Is there a passenger list showing where everyone slept that night? None exists, I am told.

A family tradition holds that my grandparents' stateroom was at the very point of collision: with no confirmation by written records, should we accept this? "Take it," says David. "That is probably true."

And so, where are their remains?

David draws in the air a form of the *Empress* as doom strikes: a hit to starboard, immediately the ship begins to list that way, with the water's weight — "*All* of the port lifeboats are now unusable" — and David's parallel palms twist to show an angle maintained all the way to her grave.

Those starboard rooms pushed by gravity into the riverbed: have they ever been explored? "So much mud is on that side that nobody has ever seen the damage," he explains. And there, presumably, my grandparents' mortal remains lie. Grim this truth may be, but I am relieved to have it.

David shows me a 1935 letter written by Captain Kendall to a woman who survived the *Empress* disaster. It was about her friend, who had drowned — "gargled salt water," in his graphic phrase. "Even under the tragic circumstances of 1914," he said, "perhaps we can get together and have a laugh."

The *Empress* inquiry relieved Kendall of responsibily for the disaster. It placed full blame on Alfred Toftenes, chief officer on the *Storstad*, for changing course in the fog and failing to summon Captain Andersen "until the mischief had been done."

Kendall became the CPR's marine superintendant at Antwerp, just before World War I brought advancing German troops into the port. Here was his old command, the *Montrose*; he packed in Belgian refugees and sailed her, with the similarly loaded *Montreal* in tow behind, across the English Channel to safety. He entered Royal Navy service and soon his command, the HMS *Calgarian*, was torpedoed by submarines at the cost of forty-nine lives. Kendall again became a marine superintendant after that war, retiring just before the next one began.

David is gripped by the letter's tone. "It's like he wanted to talk about it, get it out of his system. He was reliving it all his life."

Journalist Harry Rasky interviewed Kendall in 1959, finding him amiable. "People seem to think I'm playing a harp," he laughed. "I'm still going strong." Having what Rasky called a "sailor's gift for a good yarn," he provided his grandchildren and great-grandchildren with many stories. And at any opportunity he would recite Kipling's *If*:

> . . . *If you can fill the unforgiving minute*
> *With sixty seconds' worth of distance run,*
> *Yours is the Earth and everything that's in it,*
> *And — which is more — you'll be a Man, my son!*

Kendall died in 1964, the obituary identifying him as "the man who caught Crippen" — and giving the *Empress of Ireland* no mention. He was 88. Perhaps David and Bertha Creighton would have lived as long as he, except for that small miscalculation off Rimouski.

DIVING THE *EMPRESS*

Unlike the Titanic, *the* Empress *is lying on her side, and bulkheads within the ship have already collapsed. Many of the bones of the victims are buried under those walls, along with furniture, tools and other pieces of the ship.*

Bob Harvey, "The *Empress* will Soon be Lost,"
Ottawa *Citizen*, April 27, 1998

M Y PHONE CALL TO Stephen Brooks, a local dentist who dives the *Empress*, rings a bell: "I know that name!" He has heard about the earlier David Creighton.

"An ego dive — beyond average capabilities," says Brooks. "It became an obsession with me." Asked about the dreaded bends, he acknowledges having had them as well: "Most people get them sooner or later."

Our chat soon gets around to the salvage of teak planks from the liner in 1992 by 3091-5243 Quebec Inc. Teak, the world's most water-resistant wood, is also the most expensive — and much in demand for use in pleasure boats. Philippe Beaudry brought a court case against the company, arguing that it disturbed both the wreck and those for whom it is an underwater tomb.

The firm's lawyers answered that Canadian Pacific, back in 1914, showed little respect for the dead when the wreck was punctured to remove silver ingots. Only *loose* planks of teak were being taken, said the company's divers — reportedly twenty tons of it, more likely fifty-five. But it lost the case, and was told to pay a fine: the colossal sum of $500.

Yet the decking's removal had already caused severe structural damage, Brooks points out: tear it off, and the steel comes with it. "Now the current goes through like a sandblaster. She's falling apart."

Some $700,000 worth of nickel ingots were also coveted by 3091-5243 Quebec Inc., and to get them it might have been necessary to blow off the bow, no doubt disturbing the bodies inside. In 1998, however, appeals by marine archaeologists, museum officials, and the Salvation Army thwarted this aim: it was ruled illegal, under the Criminal Code of Canada, to interfere with human remains such as lie within the *Empress* to this day.

"Back in 1983, nobody knew about the *Empress,*" says the doctor. With several retrieved items displayed in his Burlington office, he is well-known locally for enthusiasm about the ship. "Canadian Pacific didn't care, nor the Quebec Government. Now, I'd say that fifty or sixty divers go down every summer."

When I phone Mark Reynolds, a lawyer also living in Burlington, he invites me to his office. Through a friend of a friend of a friend he learned about the *Empress,* and became an avid explorer of the wreck.

Mark Reynolds with porthole recovered from Third Class dining salon.

He recounts the first descent. "It was an eerie dive, eight hundred people down there; history took hold." His partner panicked, clinging to Mark so as to knock away his breathing apparatus, then shooting to the surface, so Mark put on a spare one and found himself alone and disoriented. Only by chance did he find a rope leading to the surface: "a handout from God!"

Mark at first used guidelines — a way out of the labyrinth, like Ariadne's thread for Theseus in Greek myth — but does so no longer. These produce a *hubris* of the deep: "There is a tendency to go just a bit farther, then you're into big trouble."

What makes museums come alive, he says, is their way of connecting individuals to the artifacts. That is why he holds the wreck in reverence. Vast quantities are now taken from the *Empress*, and he fondly remembers an earlier day — before "open season" for artifacts and heavy competition among divers. "It was all lots of fun."

A paradise for divers, at first. "Almost every room I went in was pristine — apart from filth, exactly the way it was when it sank," he recalls; one would retrieve items providing this was not destructive to the ship, nor the next diver's experience. "Then money reared its ugly head."

One day, several American divers invited Reynolds to see their video. Realizing that it showed a human skull taken from inside, he urged them to destroy the tape. "Everyone takes them," they replied — falsely, he feels, as most divers show due respect.

"The steward's cabin — there are seventy to eighty corpses in that room," Mark recalls. Pocket watches and jewellery appearing in divers' videos show that their remains had been sorted through: "They never really thought of it as a tomb."

Currents fluctuate, rearranging the silt. A jumble of human remains will be covered on one dive, fully exposed on another. This is frightening: "Divers carry tons of air in multiple tanks, but there is always a fear of running out, and dying there with them."

On a wall is Ken Marschall's magnificent painting of divers exploring the sunken *Empress* — the original, Mark having received it in gratitude for helping with the details. He regrets that the stern is inaccurately shown: "I should have explained that it was in much better shape."

A case displays *Empress* artifacts, most of them found in First Class baggage. "Figure this one out," he says, opening a container with four wooden objects the size of chess pieces. I am as baffled as Mark had been; but his wife was immediately able to assemble the parts as a candle-holder.

Here is a miniature pagoda, such as would have been conveyed on one *Empress* liner from Shanghai and on another as far as Rimouski. Efficiencies of the Canadian Pacific.

"This is the most amazing one," says Mark, handing over a beer jug. "I found it in the First Class kitchen, hanging there!" That sudden tilt, that long descent, that river-bottom impact — and still, the jug remained there on its hook.

Finally we study a dinner plate from First Class, with fine-grain fissures but still in one piece. Eighty years of immersion have impregnated these cracks with salt, which cause small bumps as it expands. He will occasionally rinse it in clear water to let the salt come out.

"I would like you to have this," says Mark. In gratitude I receive the plate, its CPR emblem pristine: physical evidence of the liner where my grandparents still lie.

I have joined, in a sense, the quest for artifacts.

David Creighton with First Class dinner plate.

PART TWO

BLESSINGS

CRAZY LIFE OF MAN

*There was some disturbance in loading the last two forward
starboard boats. A large crowd of men was pressing to get into
them. No women were around as far as I could see. I saw
Ismay, who had been assisting in the loading of the last boat,
push his way into it. It was really every man for himself.*

Titanic *survivor John Thayer, reminiscing in 1940*

FOLLOWING DISASTER THE STORSTAD was seen to have had one of
her bow anchors reddened, where it cut into human flesh within
the *Empress*. Cabin 328's number plate was later discovered on the
collier's prow, which scooped it out in praying-mantis fashion.

Rimouski's new multimedia spectacle is slated to include one
room penetrated by a replica of the *Storstad*'s prow. Some twenty-five
feet it went in, through midship cabins thought to have been
occupied by Salvationists.

Long ago, visualizing the very worst manner of death, I would
see some maze-like structure with a wall of water rushing in. I never
linked this cataclysm with the fate of my grandparents — trapped,
perhaps, in one of those smashed staterooms.

Taking Jungian analysis with the discerning Sylvia Senensky in
Guelph, I failed to mention the *Empress* until the fourth or fifth
session. "Why didn't you tell me about this?" she demanded. Sylvia
now interprets several of my traits — "an inner sense of order gives
you safety . . . being over-prepared, you remain outside the magic
and mystery" — in terms of the disaster's enduring shadow.

Sylvia's Jungian specialty is the labyrinth, that inward path
toward the Minotaurs of your life. Labyrinths are *walking meditations*
by which you sort things out: starting at the outside, making your
way to the centre of things, heading back to the normal world. She
is writing a book about this.

My own labyrinth journey has taken me into Quebec, and now
it's time to take a wider sweep of the world.

What is it like to be on a doomed ocean liner? *The Last Voyage of the Empress of Ireland* will tell the tale — and something like it is already up and running in Orlando, Florida: *Titanic — Ship of Dreams*. I take a bus down to see it.

A city guide in my motel mentions this attraction. It presents "luxury and grandeur" such as the *Titanic* boasted; and "along the way, you will share in the inspirational stories of her passengers and crew."

Titanic — Ship of Dreams is set in a Festive World Marketplace, with "over 60 of Orlando's most festive specialty shops." A rock 'n' roll bar offers "blazing pianos." Nightly entertainment is free, and by the use of coupons I will amass $200 in savings.

Next morning I set out on foot with a map inserted in the guide, but its scale is askew. Still far away after an hour, I thumb a ride and thus meet James Daughtry, a young African-American playing Motown on his cassette player.

"Are you into hip-hop?" I ask.

Advertisement for
*Titanic —
Ship of Dreams.*

Instantly he switches over to a cassette in that genre, exclaiming, "I *produce* hip-hop — I'm the *artist*, man!" James chops both hands to the beat as he sings along; thrusts them to his heart and back out; points a thumb back to himself: "*Well well?* True . . . no-brainer . . . the repertoire . . . resink the *Titanic* . . ."

Hold on — the *Titanic?* I ask for that part again, and James wheels into a parking lot to rewind the tape for me:

I'll resink the *Titanic* with a water balloon,
Rethink a hieroglyph and make it see through,
Manipulate red till it turns blue.

What's all that about? "Crazy life of man!" James laughs.

Having read vernacular poems about a black *Titanic* stoker, "Shine," I urge James to hear some Shine lyrics. The first to alert the captain yet only gaining rebuke, Shine remains blithe: "Well, that seems damned funny, it may be damned fine, but I'm gonna try to save this black ass of mine." And so on, through many comic verses.

James, in 1999, sees the *Titanic* as material not for satire but self-expression. "Allow me to just be myself, just understand me!" he explains — then gives a groan and I look up to see a pretty woman walking by, the object of his regard. "*That's* why I write songs, man!" he exclaims as we say goodbye.

I continue in a bus that speaks — "We-are-now-approaching-Wet'n'Wild!" — toward Festive World Marketplace, where I have a photo taken with three parrots on my shoulder.

I get lost in the Mediterranean Village, where families at 11 a.m. already attack lunch, but eventually find *Titanic* — *Ship of Dreams*. Rimouski should try this setup, which seems ideal for the mall's profit margin.

Awaiting entry into the attraction *per se*, visitors view a data-packed video combining sepia and colour footage: "pistons 3 1/2 stories high ... she slides into the water in only sixty-two seconds ... anchor thirty thousand pounds ... cream of Edwardian upper class ... Guggenheim, Astor ... posh First Class smoking room ... inlays of mother of pearl ..."

The soul of a machine, fine, but this tape keeps repeating itself. Retold and retold and retold and retold again — like so much of the *Titanic* mythology.

A "White Star Line attendant" is here, and I ask her about visitor response. "Little kids get hysterical, they scream and cry, they want life jackets," she says. "They yell, 'We don't want to go down with the ship,' and the parents tell them, 'It's a museum, like.'"

We are guided within by a young woman costumed as in 1912. "Aren't you glad you're First Class?" she asks, giving us the status of "investors."

Portrayed just ahead are J. Bruce Ismay, White Star's managing director; William Pirrie, who dreamed up the *Titanic* and two sister ships as leviathans, half again as big as the largest Cunard Line vessels; and J. Pierpont Morgan, the bold American financier behind the White Star Line.

A youth impersonating Ismay inevitably employs the phrase "practically unsinkable" (which appeared in a contemporary shipping journal) while explaining how she was built. Maligned for saving his own skin when the *Titanic* went down, Ismay later withdrew to an Irish retreat and would visit London only to watch ceremonial parades, anonymous among curbside crowds.

In the next room, simulating the Belfast shipyard where our liner took shape, a make-believe shipyard worker jeers, "Ye're investors, are ye!" He becomes mouthy, I carry out my big-money role by dressing him down, and a hearty shouting match ensues.

Our original guide returns, none too soon, with First Class chatter. "Did you go to *Paris?*", she asks — and then, out of character, explains to me that her task is to "keep it light." For the mood here, generally, is downbeat.

"Only yesterday a man was in tears," she adds. "At the same time as the *Titanic* sailed, his grandfather came out from Europe, Third Class — and was glad to survive the crossing and have many descendants. That man could see what it all meant."

On display is what purports to be the actual wooden sea chest of Third Officer Herbert Pitman. Yes, the same Pitman described in the 1912 U.S. Senate hearings as having captained No 5 lifeboat, with a capacity for sixty-five people and yet receiving only forty. "Now, men, we will pull towards the wreck!" he ordered at first, seeing many in need of rescue. But then he allowed the men to rest on their oars, when women protested what they saw as a "useless attempt."

Later the hearings' chairman, William Alden Smith, inquired about No. 5 boat's proximity to the dying:

> Smith: And you lay in the vicinity of that scene for about an hour?
>
> Pitman: Oh, yes; we were in the vicinity of the wreck the whole time.
>
> Smith: And drifted or lay on your oars during that time?
>
> Pitman: We drifted toward daylight, as a little breeze came up.

Smith: Did this anguish or these cries of distress die away?
Pitman: Yes; they died away gradually.

Ahead is a section of hull and gangway, where we make the fateful decision to go aboard: no tantrums this time. We hear the *Blue Danube* waltz in our First Class regions, along with gossip from another period-garbed woman: "Madeleine Astor! You know the story — only 19 and the wife of John Jacob Astor, all of 48!"

A First Class parlour suite resembles that wherein Jack Dawson, in James Cameron's *Titanic*, does the nude portrait of Rose DeWitt Bukater — here, by implication, a fictionalized Madeleine Astor.

I am interested in the dinner plates displayed ahead, on tables set amid potted palms like those abounding in the big liners. These are from the *Majestic*, I learn — "but White Star used them interchangably on its ships."

The *Titanic*'s Grand Staircase, perfectly reconstructed! With its glass dome, and its clock reading 10:30! A fellow investor asks what significance that time holds — and is readily informed, "No significance at all!"

Second Officer Charles Lightoller was transfixed by the sight of "that cold, green water, crawling its ghostly way up that staircase." I find myself wondering how such effects could be replicated in the ultimate 3-D museum.

The reconstituted bridge has a steering wheel for us to turn, and footage of an iceberg straight ahead. Through video magic, we feel the pain of our brand new liner goring herself to death. We hear sounds of ice and steel grinding together. Interior shot of water pouring in along the torn area, exterior shot of bubbles escaping: very effective.

We step into chilled air approximating that of the early hours on April 15, 1912. The replicated stars are brilliant. "Be brave," a voice utters; "no matter what happens, be brave." It is that of Dr. W.T. Minahan to Mrs Minahan — according to Walter Lord in *A Night to Remember*, chapter 4 — "as he stepped back with the other men."

"It's all right, little girl; you go and I'll stay a while." Dan Marvin to his bride, same chapter. "He blew her a kiss as she entered the boat." *Women and children first*: one of the main governing myths.

A sudden *whoosh*: 12:45, first of the distress rockets — four of which are seen and ignored by the nearby *Californian*. Hope dwindles. Below our deck is the appearance of ocean water, black, its temperature 28 degrees Fahrenheit — which, said a survivor who dived in, felt like "a thousand knives" driven into the body.

"Are there any more women before this boat goes?" another voice inquires.

At 1:55 Boat No. 4, the last of all, was entered by five-months-pregnant Madeleine Astor. Her husband stood waving, smiling, before going down to liberate their Airedale dog, Kitty — whom she later saw running about on the fast-settling deck. Surely the most graphic image of inevitable death that night.

The deck has a projecting section of what appears to be a chapel, with arched windows. Now beneath those bright stars, we catch the melody famously believed to have been played by Wallace Hartley's string group: "Nearer My God to Thee."

The greatest of all *Titanic* clichés. Salvation Army associations must be at work to give it such an impact on my feelings, here at this mall attraction.

The next room offers horrifying video footage: a funnel toppling, the ship explosively breaking in two. An engineering marvel then noses down in the long descent.

Passenger Charlotte Collyer finally heard two dull, heavy explosions, "as if below the surface the *Titanic* broke into two before my eyes." And so it was, the colossus cracking apart with living souls inside — wrecked machinery, like that of the world's armies soon to wage all-out war.

A photo shows lifeboats being picked up by the *Carpathia*, whose passengers beheld "the awesome sight of a huge ice field with twenty small boats over a four-mile area."

In the gift shop, where an authentic replica of *Titanic* deck chair sells for $1,200, I chat with a Venezuelan visitor, a Pentecostal. "The *Titanic*: that's about having the Gospel in their heart and trying to love other people," he remarks. "Inside to outside!"

CHOCOLATE *TITANIC* SHIP

This book is really about the last night of a small town.
Walter Lord, *A Night to Remember*

A drive to Newport News, Virginia, takes me to the sprawling Mariner's Museum. Recently it held an exhibit titled *Titanic: Fortune & Fate*. Now I meet Heather Friedle, an archivist who helped to organize the show.

It told of episodes recorded in survivors' diaries and letters — and yet, as Heather points out, *Titanic's* fictional tale of Jack and Rose held centre stage. She hands me a "Questions and Answers" leaflet given out at the exhibit:

11. **Were the characters of Jack and Rose actual, real-life Titanic passengers?**

No. James Cameron's Rose and Jack are both typical of the passengers who would have been travelling in first and third class respectively.

"We were *swamped* with visitors," Heather recalls. "We had the tickets randomly printed with *Titanic* passengers' names — and of course, all the kids were shouting, 'I wanna be Jack!' or 'I wanna be Rose!'"

She has heard about the *Empress of Ireland*. "A tragic story, but completely overshadowed by the *Titanic* disaster," she says. "The first one lessens the impact. And think of all that press the *Titanic* had before sailing. England to New York — it couldn't be any better, that huge ship entering the harbour. People in New York were dying to see it come in."

In Washington I visit the 1931 Women's Titanic Memorial, at 6th and N Streets SE, officially described as a marble "figure of Heroism, a man of noble proportions, fifteen feet high, the face, arms, and whole posture of the body exemplifying a willing sacrifice, a smiling welcome to death."

A gala theatrical fundraiser was held for the memorial. "When our children look on that monument," said one actor, "they will say, 'Thank God I belong to that race which in the hour of sorest trial said, *Ladies first.*" That is, the *Anglo-Saxon* race.

At midnight on each anniversary of the ship's sinking, I am told, tuxedo-clad men of the media trades here give a toast to those who made the "willing sacrifice." On this sultry afternoon the memorial's isolation is a plus for two lovers, joined in a lengthy embrace.

Women's *Titanic*
Memorial.
(David Creighton)

The memorial was moved from a site now occupied by the Kennedy Center, where *Titanic — A New Musical* happens to be playing tonight. I take in the show along with another of those ocean-liner Last Suppers, offered at its Roof Top Restaurant. As in Quebec City, there is a novelty dessert:

Chocolate Titanic Ship, Filled with White Chocolate Mousse, Lemon Sorbet Iceberg, Caramel Sauce

The meal, by no means as convivial as at the Château Frontenac's round tables, gives opportunity for the chef, who is new and unknown:

self-expression once again. I ask my server whether these *Titanic* dinners might be considered ghoulish. "Make it more real-life!" he exclaims. "Teach a history lesson!"

Titanic — a New Musical, Act One. J. Bruce Ismay goads Captain Smith into ever-faster rates of speed — twenty-one knots, twenty-two knots, twenty-three knots, twenty-four knots — to sharpen White Star's competitive edge. Doom is foreshadowed by the tune "Autumn," sung to a manic engine-pulse as the iceberg is struck: dark soul of a machine.

Act Two. A tea cart rolls slowly across the room, simulacrum of the *Titanic's* fate. Ismay prevaricates still: *Not even God himself could sink this ship.* First lifeboat drill of the trip, "a mere formality." Captain Smith musing now on "innocent folk, dreaming their dreams."

The still-lovelorn Isador and Ida Straus exchange toasts: "To us!" This very chocolate-*Titanic* moment garners huge applause. And what a great farewell scene these two were able to create, unlike my ancestors.

By expert stagecraft, the boat dramatically rears and sinks. There was to have been a finale showing the wreck being revisited by a yellow submarine, à la James Cameron, but this never took shape.

Hannah Koltuv of Partisan Pictures, in New York, has phoned for help in a documentary about the *Empress of Ireland* and other ships for the Public Broadcasting System. "Right now, we have a very general idea of what we're doing," says she, referring to "floating palaces of the gilded age." *Lost Liners* is the tentative title.

So here I am today at Partisan's workspace, offering five binders of *Empress* material. Her attention falls on one with all the photos: Who is this, and what is that, and where was this taken?

In our *Empress* coverage, says Hannah, the Salvation Army will be front and centre. She and I share the experience of drifting from our religious moorings. "Judaism — now I wonder what all that was about," she remarks.

Peter Schnall, the company's founder, explains that "Partisan" is political in a way now largely forgotten: activism without any one ideology. Work he previously did for *National Geographic* magazine, in undersea-exploration coverage, is continued here on an independent basis.

I also visit the Salvation Army's West 14th Street executive headquarters, with its gilded bust of the Founder, William Booth. A famed passage from his last address, at London's Albert Hall in 1912, is spelled out in large letters:

> *While there is a drunkard left,*
> *While there is a poor lost girl*
> *upon the streets,*
> *While there remains one dark soul*
> *without the light of God*
> *I'll fight*
> *I'll fight to the very end.*

William Booth required obedience to God's will, a concept stemming from ancient Israel. God was seen to be deeply concerned with human ways. Salvationists, similarly, must quell self-centredness to share others' pain.

The building is dedicated to the "vision and courage" of Booth's daughter, Evangeline, commander-in-chief over the US Salvationists for thirty years. In England, she had gained rapport with the downfallen by donning worn attire and peddling goods on the street — thus developing themes for "illustrated lectures" as announced on billboards wherever she performed:

> *Miss Booth in Rags*
> *Will tell the Tale*
> *of a Broken Heart*
> *And Sing the Song of Love!*

These caused a sensation; as one reporter stated, "The audience saw them as if portrayed by a great tragedienne." Women evangelists in that era won the kind of acclaim given today to a Céline Dion or a Shania Twain. Going on to serve briefly as commander in Canada, she was known for wearing a red wig while leading parades upon a white horse.

Nobody here knows of the *Empress* disaster; but for Eva Booth it produced trauma. Later sailing to England aboard the *Olympic*, sister ship of the *Titanic*, Eva was "obliged to keep to her cabin throughout the whole voyage," said the *War Cry*. "The loss of her Canadian comrades had contributed in no small degree to her overwrought condition."

I drive to Indian Orchard, Massachusetts, where the Titanic Historical Society's small museum is found. Fortified by a Cream-of-Wheat breakfast at the Pleasant Snack Bar ("A Restaurant Where It Feels Like Home"), I go on to Henry's Jewelry Shop, where images of the Virgin Mary in the window bespeak the Catholicism of the Society's founder, Ed Kamuda. His museum is in behind.

Barbara Kamuda.
(David Creighton)

Here Barbara Kamuda tells how her brother started his matchless collection of *Titanic* artifacts after seeing J Arthur Rank's 1953 film *A Night to Remember* in their father's movie theatre — the Grand, just across the street. Ed was fascinated by a booklet given by the Rank organization to each theatre owner. It listed names and addresses of survivors then living, and he wrote a letter to each one.

"My brother did this as a labour of love, not for cash," says Barbara. Among the many replies he received was a 1964 letter from

Frederick Fleet, the lookout who sighted the iceberg. A sketch shows the scene: First Sight and Impact.

"Thank heaven for pack rats," Barbara laughs. Ed's research meant a lot to James Cameron, who returned the favour by dressing Ed and his wife in period costume for a brief deck scene in the film: displayed here is an enlargement of the frame.

Society members preserved *Titanic*-related items otherwise lost — notably a White Star flag on the liner *Queen Mary*. It would have been torn up for rags, had a THS member not placed the relic under his shirt and conveyed it to safety.

"Come in and join the crowd!" Barbara genially cries to people newly arrived to see the museum. Many wish to be *shown through*, she tells me. Or ask, "How long does it take?" To which she will reply, "Well, how much do you want to know?"

She is justifiably proud of the THS flag once flown by Robert Ballard over the *Britannic*, sister ship of the *Titanic*. Here is a styrofoam coffee cup placed by him near the *Titanic*, and promptly reduced to the size of a thimble. "That's 3 1/2 tons of pressure per square inch," she explains.

When visitors ask who was responsible for what happened, Barbara will reply, "No one." Her attention is upon "the way things were done" back in that era, when "gentlemen actually gave up their seats."

She holds high regard for the self-sacrificial Captain Smith, who was "responsible for every single life aboard. "And from the skipper on down it was "honourable," she affirms. "That's totally changed now, not much respect any more. Today, it's every man for himself."

In *Going Down with the Old Canoe*, Steven Biel quotes a White Star vice-president on chivalric self-sacrifice: this is "a matter of courtesy extended by the stronger to the weaker on land as well as on the sea." Yet the *Titanic's* male passengers, Biel argues, might have seen poorer odds in a lifeboat voyage than in staying with the ship.

I venture to ask Barbara for her take on Biel — notably, this motive as the true reason why those tuxedoed gentlemen "stood back" from lifeboat rescue. "Well, the women were tired, it was cold, and getting into that tiny little thing was no picnic," she reflects. "But the men — standing back, that's the way they wanted to meet death."

ANOTHER *TITANIC*
DISASTER

Oh, they loaded up the boats so very far from shore
but the rich refused to associate with the poor.
So they put the poor below,
where they were the first to go.
It was sad when the great ship went down.
Old tune

WHEN THE *Empress of Ireland* sank, everybody compared it with the one that went down before. London's *Daily Mail* headlined its story, "ANOTHER *TITANIC* DISASTER" — the first of many papers to use the phrase.

"I know that the great difference was in the fact that we were afloat only a very few minutes after the collision," said Major Frank Morris, an *Empress* survivor. "Yet there was no panic on the *Ireland* and in that respect it must have been very much like the *Titanic* catastrophe."

On May 30, 1914 the *Globe* gave an *Empress* viewpoint by a Londoner, J. Fergus Duncan. "He saw men standing back ready to face their doom after they handed over a life-belt or preserver to a woman or child," it states — but later *in the same article* Duncan is quoted as saying, "From the first it was every man for himself, and men, women, and children made the most of it."

One difference is that land was well within view; so the June 1 *Globe* says that a "Miss I. Townsend, a New Zealand girl of seventeen years, noted in athletics," dived in and covered a full mile before being picked up, in excellent health. "I did not dare look back," she is quoted as saying, "lest what I might see would unnerve me."

Yet a swim of that length surely would have taken her well away from where she might be seen, let alone picked up. More plausible is the story about a "Tiria Townshend" (the correct name) stating that she clung to an empty suitcase while an acquaintance helped her to struggle out of a sodden overcoat that drained strength away. The other account came, presumably, from a reporter's imagination.

The Canadian Pacific's first disaster statement, given in the May 31 *Globe*, told that the *Empress* had been rammed "in such a manner as to tear the ship from the middle to the screw." This seems to have been pure guesswork, echoing what was then assumed about the *Titanic* — that doom resulted from a continuous gash made by the fateful iceberg.

The *Globe* looked for heroes and found one in the hardworking Dr. James Grant, who "takes a place with the youthful Marconi operator who stayed at his post when the *Titanic* was foundering."

The *Globe* was also quick to assign hero-and-villain roles to the two captains. "BRAVE KENDALL STUCK TO HIS POST," it says on May 30; "he behaved like a true British sailor while his ship sank under his feet." Kendall "stood on his bridge as the ship went down, and was picked up by one of his boats."

In the June 1 *Globe* one heading, "CAPTAIN KENDALL PROVED HIMSELF TO BE A HERO / Stuck to the Ship, Picked up by Lifeboat, Rescued Scores of Persons," is placed near another that reads, "STORSTAD'S CAPTAIN DECLINED INTERVIEW / Would Not Be Seen When His Boat Reached Quebec."

The *Globe* is still at it on June 2: "A GRAVE CHARGE AGAINST ANDERSEN / Montreal KC Says Storstad Captain Was Indifferent / His Statement Corroborated by That of Other Survivors — Declare That Storstad Crew Seemed to Treat the Whole Thing as Matter of Course."

Character types similar to those on the *Titanic* were found — a counterpart to Molly "Unsinkable" Brown being Sherbrooke society queen Ethel Paton. She put on her best attire, complete with diamonds, and rolled off the deck right into Lifeboat 1, which was narrowly missed by the forward funnel when it crashed down alongside. Ethel, having taken along a sewing bag with nail scissors, used them on the *Storstad* to fashion a pillow case into clothing for an eight-year-old girl orphaned that night.

The mangled body of the *Titanic's* John Jacob Astor was identified by initials on his shirt; that of *Empress* victim Sir Henry Seton-Karr by a handkerchief bearing his initials. He was said to have pressed his life-jacket on a fellow-passenger, Merton Darling, as the ship began to turn over. "Go on, man, take it, I'll try to get another," said the sportsman before retiring to his cabin, to be seen alive no more. His body was recovered 40 miles downstream from where the *Empress* sank.

Elderly Isador and Ida Straus famously refused to separate at No 8 lifeboat; and high-profile conjugal affection was noted on the

Empress as well: husband-and-wife actors Laurence Irving and Mabel Hackney were cast as the doomed lovers.

"Irving was kissing his wife as the boat went down," said fellow-passenger Frederick Abbott, "and they were clasped in each other's arms." A pathetic story about their remains, later questioned, told that Irving's hand held a scrap of her nightdress.

On the *Titanic* only one woman, Rosa Abbott, went "down with the ship" and survived, but on the *Empress* that horror was experienced by several survivors. Mary Attwell and her husband, Major George Attwell, were submerged three times — "kicked, struck and clutched at by numbers of desperate human beings" — before reaching a lifeboat, "more dead than alive when pulled aboard." All entered the water, the major recalled, "with one common consent and an agonizing shout."

OLD TIMES ON
TROUT CREEK

To go down among the perishing crowds is your duty. Your happiness henceforth will consist in sharing their pain, your crown in wearing their cross, and your heaven in going to the very jaws of hell to rescue them.
William Booth, *War Cry*, June 20, 1885

WHILE I CONTINUE THROUGH New Hampshire and Maine, the car radio gives reports on burial-at-sea rites for John F. Kennedy's namesake son, killed in a plane crash. Taped remarks by his assassinated father lend apt comment: *We all came from the sea, we are tied to the ocean. And when we go back to the sea — whether it is to sail or to watch it — we are going back from whence we came.*

Phone-in comments describe sudden loss by misadventure: "There's just despair afterwards . . . you don't ever forget it . . . the pain never goes away . . . time is not a guaranteed healer."

This sets a mood for my visit to St. Stephen, New Brunswick, where David and Bertha Creighton served the Salvationist cause. Their daughter Edith was born here in 1895, nineteen years before they drowned. The pain of loss overtook Edith at each anniversary of the sinking, as she would become physically ill. This happened for the rest of her days.

Big photos mounted beside the Saint Croix River show this town in the 1890s, when my grandparents served its needs. Lots of mud. Rough-looking people on the main street. And sailing ships, both sides of the river.

The St. Stephen Army corps, I learn, is no more. Jane, at the Pizza Delight, tells me about going downtown on Saturday nights in the fifties and hearing a small Army band. "The Sally Ann and a hot dog cart — that was our entertainment," she laughs. "They moved from one end of town to the other as the night went on. Pretty good music."

Next morning at the Tim Hortons I get more details from Jim, another long-time resident: "A tambourine, a drum, a horn. They had uniforms. Their pot was out. The church at that time was

Mounted photo in St. Stephen, New Brunswick.
(David Creighton)

downtown, where the new Royal Bank went up. I almost think they had a small lodging place as well."

I mention that my grandfather once served here, striving to keep the citizenry on straight paths. "Well, that was their calling, and still is," Jim observes. "This used to be a fairly wild little town until it mellowed out — whisky-running during Prohibition and all that."

Looking for signs of wildness today in St. Stephen — known as "Canada's Chocolate Town" for the Ganong factory operating here — I come upon a sign at the Old Town Tavern:

> *Advance tickets for BOYS NIGHT OUT*
> *4 female exotic dancers*
> *back by popular demand*

Salvationists, like those of Methodist persuasion, would frown on such earthly joys. But the Army, "Methodism boiling over," drew many for whom older denominations seemed out-of-date, lifeless.

"It was the church of those who had few claims to respectability," notes S.D. Clark in his classic study, *Church and Sect in Canada*. "The

Army worker had no hesitation in stopping to minister to the drunkard, ex-criminal, or prostitute on the street."

Salvationists most recently had "a small little building, like a modular home, on the outskirts," says Jim. "It closed only a few years ago." I drive out by the railway tracks, and there it is, under a maple with a FOR SALE sign nailed to its trunk: the St. Stephen Army hall at its final location.

At Saint John, my grandfather first learned about the Salvation Army. Here, hoping to find historical perspective at the handsome New Brunswick Museum, I ask to see exhibits on immigration, sailing ships, religion, race, crime, urban texture, class, economic growth, and the like.

The girl gives a cheery reply: "We don't have anything about that on display, right now — but, it's in storage!"

The next best thing is to visit a downtown square where David first noted high enthusiasm in a "Blood and Fire army" — Christ's redemptive blood, the Holy Spirit's fire — that ventured to "fire the first shot on King Square." A video crew is active here today, filming two young cops with the square's 1909 bandstand as backdrop.

Here in April 1885 this revolutionary force, comprising only Staff-Captain Young and four women, was seen hot-gospelling. David, soberly raised as a Methodist, later witnessed their invasion of Sussex, his home town: "The girls I thought rather light and happy to be earnest Christians, while the man amused me by taking two steps at a bound when ascending the stairs."

At the present corps, a barebones structure on Waterloo Street, I chat with Major Larry Bridger about Saint John's early citadels. "This is the latest of at least five locations," he says; "in your grandfather's day, it might have been on Charlotte beside King Square."

The Army again holds open-air meetings on this elegant square, he adds: "Just started this year — had to get permission, of course; not everywhere can you go out on the streets these days."

David, becoming seriously ill in 1885, promised God to "do right" if spared. His spiritual quest now took a clear direction. In a ledger book serving as a journal, my grandfather described his entry into Salvationism and a new life, somewhere in Saint John.

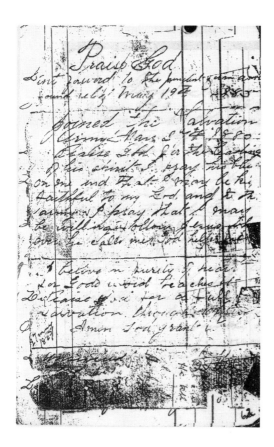

Journal entry by David
Creighton, 1885.

Praise God

*Went forward to the penitent form and found relief May 19th
1885. Joined the Salvation Army May 27th 1885. Praise God
for the lashing of his spirit. I pray his blessing on me and that I
may be his, faithful to my God and to the army. I pray that I
may be willing to follow Jesus wherever he calls me. God help me.*

Here is a kind of charter for my family, a Salvationist covenant
with the divine.

In the hall, downstairs, I leaf through a recent *War Cry*: "Cocaine
Was My God"; "The Need for Revival is Urgent"; "Barriers Between
Us and God"; Part 3 of a series titled "Holy Spirit: Person and
Power" by the current commissioner.

There is a *War Cry* memoir by David giving more details of his
conversion. Several men awaiting orders to serve in the North-West

Rebellion had come to the hall, "mostly well-filled with the Devil," and their raucous spirit gripped him. "I felt like cursing God," said David, who "had almost to hold on to the seat to keep from going out."

Then, those wishing to be converted were asked to hold up their hands. "It was now or never," he said. An inner voice gave encouragement, and he accepted the divine will: "I felt no great exhilarating joy, only a positive assurance of my acceptance in the Beloved." Thus he *found relief*.

The Army's blood-and-fire flag is mounted here alongside that of Canada. To join the Army, converts stand between the two and repeat Booth's Methodist-derived doctrines.

Then came David's first Holiness meeting, at which "pure living" was preached through a text from *Romans*: "Shall we continue in sin that grace may abound? God forbid!" Now, as the perspiration "came out in great drops," he testified to "full" salvation, on Earth as in Heaven.

"Lord open a way for me," he prayed, "and help me to do Thy will in all things." He went on to officership, serving for twenty-nine years until being *promoted to glory* on the *Empress*.

Salvation Army corps at Saint John, New Brunswick.
(David Creighton)

Three years after his St. Stephen posting, David turned from evangelism to social service such as goes on today at the Army's shelter on St. James Street. Here I am permitted to roam the ground floor: a lounge, stuffy with last night's bedding; and a cafeteria, with a Dickensian array of faces. A "Mission Statement," no bigger than a license plate, gives the only spiritual reference to be found here:

*The Saint John Booth Centre, inspired by the love of Christ,
provides shelter for the homeless, opportunity for a new
beginning, in a caring community.*

When I ask an employee how the Army functions here today, he
takes me outside for a frank discussion. "There are some really smart
people staying here — they want out so badly, they can almost taste
it," I am told. "But on job applications, to put down 'Booth Centre' is
fatal because they take it to mean that there's no potentiality."

The Army's aims are sincere, but funding is low. And many of
these people never advance, "opportunity for a new beginning" being
illusory to a painful degree.

I continue past Sussex to a ghost town, named Creightonville. Here
Michael Creighton, from Downpatrick in Northern Ireland, settled
after being "transported," it is said, for shooting a hare.

Transported for shooting a hare: in 1825, at 23, he started a new life.
Required by law to choose between North America and Australia, he
decided on the former.

Michael Creighton thus became our clan's Canadian forefather.

In Biblical terms this errant youth might be seen as an outcast
from Eden, thorns and thistles overrunning the land of exile. But
here he prospered. "It was Michael's custom to always wear a white
shirt," great-grandson Wilfred writes, "which might indicate he
considered himself a bit above the ordinary farmer." In Ireland he
had something to do with horses, and could have enjoyed a status
that he now wished to regain.

Creightonville Cemetery is about all that remains of the pioneer
community. The one-room Methodist church that was raised here
by Michael has been demolished, but the patriarch himself lies on
the slope above, alongside his wife Jane.

A daughter, Mary Ann, in old age wrote a letter giving a few
details about the patriarch. "When he was a child going to school he
played many times on St. Patrick's grave," she states. Shooting the
hare — a forbidden act for "all persons, except Landlords and their
sons" — Michael made his way to Saint John and there became
engaged to Jane Magee. He went to Boston for three years, amassed
a sum of £500, returned to marry Jane, and brought her here in "the
first wagon that ever entered the place."

Jane was dark, tall, and of slight build. These physical traits, and Michael's reddish complexion, are seen in the clan today.

Jane's mother, who had turned Methodist while her parents held true to Anglicanism, was beaten by them for this effrontery. She and Michael now ingrained their five children in the tenets of evangelical faith.

William was the most energetic of these offspring. When neighbours came to help mow the hay, he would be placed prominently on the field to set a pace for others to follow. Yet he fell victim to childhood curiosity, says Wilfred, while playing one day with his sister Mary Ann: "They were just little youngsters and got into talking about the axe lying there and one or the other using it to chop off a finger. Before long William put his hand on a block of wood and Mary Ann promptly cut off his index finger."

This victim of "aggravated" assault went on, all the wiser, to preside as a much-respected justice of the peace. "Squire," they called him.

William married Isabella Law, a woman almost fanatical in her religious devotion. David, her son, recalled Isabella's "singing and personal talks as she toiled over her work." There were hymns — "As on the Cross the Saviour hung," "God moves in a mysterious way" — and dire Scripture texts: *The angels shall come forth and sever the wicked from the just and shall cast them into a furnace of fire; there shall be wailing and gnashing of teeth.*

Mulling over this today, one might question Isabella's sanity. But a pioneer milieu, where forests had to be felled and crops tended in the face of starvation, would readily consign slackers and rogues to perdition. "The backwoods farm population had no strong sense of social status," states S.D. Clark. "The convert was made to feel that he was one of a very privileged group; the person unconverted was the abandoned wretch, leading a solitary existence without the benefit of faith."

As country-music tunes flow from a nearby home, I read worn texts citing heavenly reward and the blood of Christ. And here is an urn-topped marker naming David and Bertha Creighton — a memorial, of course, the bodies never having been found:

DROWNED IN RIVER
ST. LAWRENCE
MAY 29, 1914

Grave marker for David and Bertha
Creighton, Creightonville,
New Brunswick. (David Creighton)

WHEN EMPRESS OF IRELAND WENT DOWN

Wilfred's history says much about the man he called "Father," about eccentric kinfolk of many kinds. But the *Empress* disaster goes unmentioned in this account, which concludes with the story of a dog who defended a dead cow. Something humourous. This may have had allegorical meaning for Wilfred, but I doubt it.

He tells how David, during boyhood, once was lauded for strenuous potato-gathering and began parading around the kitchen, only to fall through the basement's trap door — right onto the potatoes. This experience served in later years to illustrate a moral: "Pride goeth before a fall." For such lapses, William once took the boy into a stable alone to pray especially for him.

David moved off the farm to enter the tintype-photo trade, travelling in a covered van. William, against his better judgment, lent the lad several hundred dollars. When the enterprise failed, David was humbled that his father "did not reproach me, but offered further assistance." Methodism had its tender side.

Also listed on this stone is a brother, Herbert, "aged 2 years & 8 mos" at the time of death — which aroused in David "a desire to return to God that I might meet him in heaven." Yet when revival services were later held at the Methodist Church and David was expected to set an example, he "did little but smile at the prayers, tears and groans of the other seekers."

Later, at 21, he was swept away by the Salvation Army's fervour and joined within a few days. In what must have been a momentous change, William soon followed his son into the Salvation Army, together with all but one of his offspring.

A fine 1912 group portrait shows David amid his parents and siblings. He wrote to his brothers before departure on the *Empress*, requesting care for the younger children if anything were to go amiss. They followed his wishes in 1914, two becoming foster parents at opposite ends of Canada. So the family was broken up forever.

Charles Wilfred, standing at left, became an Army officer and married Lottie Lowry (not in the photo). It was they who received four-year-old Cyrus, destined to die young. Lottie saw the boy as a gift following upon disaster, "and we opened our hearts to him, and he has lived there, giving joy and sunshine until he had filled every corner."

Eight-year-old Arthur was received by Henry, (upper right) and his wife Alice, (sitting below). Henry also served the Army as an officer: "Seeing how happy religion made his elder brother David," said the *War Cry*, Henry "did valiant work, leading many to lay all at the feet of the Crucified One." He persevered in various Maritimes corps, then felt a change of heart and gave up officership, becoming sergeant-major at the Sussex citadel.

Jenny, lower left beside Isabella, served the Army before joining the Pentecostals, which had an orchestra; "and they sure whoop it up in the songs," Wilfred once reported.

Cyrus Senior, to William's right, was the only one never to become a Salvationist — nor did he marry, frankly regretting "the advantages, trials or blessings which fate and the girls denied me." He watched the stock market, garnering a small fortune.

David Creighton with siblings and parents, 1912.

Nearby are burial spaces of the Law family. David Law, after whom my grandfather was named, descended from the Scots-Ulster New Brunswick clan that produced a British prime minister, Canadian-born Andrew Bonar Law.

Law is known for having carried sackloads of grain on his back to be ground at the mill. He was only 19 on marrying Sarah Chambers in 1834. Shortly his father arrived from Ireland to claim David's wages, the youth not having reached the age of 21. Or so the story goes.

Law prospered sufficiently to leave $500 in his will for maintenance of the Creightonville church. A generous gift for the time — and yet one grandchild is known to have remarked, "Far better if he'd left it for his own family." What became of the money, nobody knows.

By car I cross Trout Creek on Creightonville's covered bridge — or "kissing bridge," in touristic idiom — to drive out the Urney Road in search of the Law property. An elderly man tells me that Laws farmed, until recently, at the Urney Road's far end.

And here is David Law's handsome eight-room house, with a gazebo added by its new non-farming owners. Isabella here became well-versed in tillage from infancy. "As a child her mother would hand her a basket with some cut up potatoes," Wilfred recalled, "and tell her to put a piece in any loose earth around a tree stump."

This was pioneers' toil, breaking in new land, yet my great-great-grandmother Sarah Law lived into the twentieth century. At family gatherings she would assume an imperial presence, sitting amid many descendants in a large upholstered chair.

Nearby Waterford, in its days as a stopover on the stagecoach run between Saint John and Moncton, had no fewer than five places licensed for liquor — but not in any would you find Michael Creighton, for whom drinking and other earthly pleasures could lead to damnation.

None of the taverns have survived. "And no stores of any kind," a resident informs me, "except for that blacksmith shop there." *Blacksmith?* "Yes — Arthur DeForest, he's in that shed just about any day in summer. Built a bed for someone last year, from scratch. He's 86 now."

I am directed to the immaculate home where Arthur and his wife Laura receive me in their living room. Laura still has very beautiful eyes, and I am conscious of her being conscious of my consciousness of her — an esteem such as she must have enjoyed for some eighty years by now.

We chat about old times on Trout Creek. "Sawmills, gristmills — God, there was a gristmill right in Waterford," he says, with awe. "Run by *water.*"

Arthur was the very man who demolished the Creightonville church, I now learn. "Closed up for a long time," he recalls. "Wasn't any use — tore it down, cleaned up the mess." Other places of worship will meet a similar fate, it seems: "The Myers church — they have only three members, a minister comes in every two weeks."

He puts the blame on competing attractions. "Lots of people on those ski runs, not in church." And agriculture falls off at the same time: "Farmers are getting limited, too."

Arthur produces a photo of his father's general store, taken around 1900. The men shown alongside would have heard my grandfather, perhaps, when he brought a Salvationist message to the community on September 10, 1885.

"Opened a meeting at Waterford," David wrote in his diary. "Living souls out for pardon and professed to be saved by the blood." Some 280 early letters sent to him survive, including some from Joseph Gulliver, a friend of David's brother Henry.

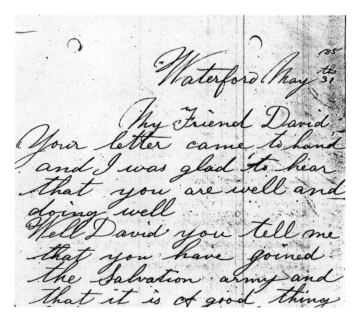

Letter from Joseph W. Gulliver, May 31, 1885.

In a letter from the pre-Army era, Show Days and farm girls are cited by Gulliver as sources of interest.

Waterford
Sept 17 1884
Dear friend

*. . . Henry Creighton and me went last sunday to find ourselves
some girls but did not find any to suit us so I think that we will
go to Mr. William Adair and we will find some there.*

*I have taken a great shine to that one you had Show Day and
I think I can hold a pretty good hand. I am going to try
anyhow, for try never was beat yet. There have been no sprees
around here this long time but they will commence now we are
almost done harvesting. . . .*

No more at present from **Joseph W. Gulliver**

David's conversion meant a remodelled self — shunning this
world's delights, setting a course toward heaven — while for his
acquaintances, life simply went on. Gulliver, told of David's eager
new commitments, laboured to give an inoffensive reply:

Waterford
Oct 6th 1885
Dear Friend David

*There is a great many people around here that don't think much of
the Salvation Army. But there is some people that can't be pleased
but for my part I think the Army is good in some ways but there is
some parts of it and I don't know what to think of it myself just
now but perhaps I will think different after a while. . . .*

Joseph W. Gulliver

The Sussex Sawmill, owned by Irving Forest Products, occupies what
had been the area's best farmland. It is beautiful as well, stretching
down to the Kennebecasis River. William Creighton bought this
farm after his parents' death, and once I saw where foundations of
the farmhouse were enclosed by a white picket fence.

"That's all gone now," I am told by an employee, who graciously
finds me an aerial view of the land under our feet. "Sonny Morrow —
we bought the land from him," he remarks, "— Sonny lives just over on
the next line."

I drive to the home of this genial man, who sold out in 1973.

"Father wasn't able to work, we couldn't get help, milking sixty head was too hard — then the Irvings came in and wanted to buy and I said yes," he explains. "I often wished I hadn't."

When the Creightons sold the farm at auction, in 1918, Sonny's grandfather bought the property.

"The place was crowded with teams, 37 sat down to dinner in the house, the rest was served outside with bread, butter and tea," said eleven-year Arthur in a mournful letter. "Our fancy double-seated carriage was sold for a $1.50. Ha! some price, but he only took the wheels. We are now in grandfather's side of the house, the men who bought the farm are living in the other side."

When Sonny's father and uncle later purchased the farm, they too lived in that other section. "I was born there," he recalls.

And was this the best farmland around? "The best in New Brunswick!" he exclaims. "You couldn't plough that deep anywhere else. Flat, no hills. There wasn't a stone on it."

When Wilfred was young, rural beauty here cast its spell during visits to Grandfather William: "it just seemed life together moved smoothly along." Once when David joined them, an idyllic memory was forged:

> I recall the three of us crossing the road and entering a trail in the bush seeking blueberries and hearing, then looking and seeing a hen partridge with her chicks scattering for cover. And then there was a clear, little stream rushing along to pass under a log in the fence, leaving a large bunch of white froth on it.

The Sussex farm became linked with a time before the *Empress*, before the proliferation of machines that could kill.

It was William who best expressed the clan's feelings about the disaster, told in a 1915 letter to my father. The message is not always clear, but expresses love and concern. William reminds his namesake "to ask <u>God every day</u> to <u>help you</u> to choose the better way that you may be able to escape the evils of this world."

Sussex April 23 1915
My Dear Grandson Willie

I have been thinking much of you and also all of you since that terrible disaster that robbed you of your Father and

> *Mother. It was a thing to be left to contend your way so young without Father or Mother. I am pleased to hear you getting along so well when I think of you all left to battle with the difficulties of this life. . . .*

The local tourist-information centre is located in Sussex's old rail station. Arthur, a keen hockey player on the high school's team, would have often passed through the depot on his way to and from games at other New Brunswick communities.

After gaining success with the Canadian Pacific back in Toronto, Arthur would visit Sussex economically on his railway pass. As "the local boy who did well," he won a modest fame in this closely knit community.

Once, as a family man, Arthur bought an expensive wheelbarrow at a friend's hardware store. But he forgot that liquid funds had dwindled, and could not return the item without making this fact

Arthur Creighton (middle, second from left) with Sussex High School hockey team, circa 1918.

plain. So he kept it, and the family later laughed about how they had to tighten their belts on the long homeward trip.

Entering Prince Edward Island in darkness, I drive toward my mother's Tryon homelands and luckily find a room at the Riverview Tourist Home. Ancestor-hunting brings me to these parts, I explain. And who are your people? The Leas. The Leas — did you know that a Richard Charles Lea, whose grandfather came out from Lincolnshire, built this home in 1880?

Unbelievable: this means that my maternal grandmother, once Lydia Lea, grew up in the very place I chanced upon. She must have set foot in the big new house at the age of 14. Opposite on the river's west bank, a shipbuilding industry thrived on the same principle as elsewhere in the Maritimes: cut down the trees and carve them into hulls.

Both of Lydia's grandparents, William Lea and Elizabeth Leard, were brought overseas by their parents and lived into her lifetime. This means that I knew a grandmother who knew ancestors arriving here in Napoleon's era. Such is the span of time.

The next morning I visit *Anne of Green Gables* territory — Cavendish Boardwalk, Cavendish Trail Rides, Cavendish Tourist Mart & Coin Laundry — and press on past these enchantments to the Park Corner farmhouse of Lucy Maud Montgomery's happiest memory. Eight years younger than my grandmother, she was married here at the age of 37. By that time Lydia, the wife of Charlottetown *Guardian* publisher J.P. Hood, had had three children and the union was falling apart.

Maud felt deep sexual passion only once, while teaching school in Lydia's south-shore region. It was with one of the Leards. And thus, had she not fended him off, a Montgomery might have been interleaved on my mother's family tree.

Instead, she went on to write the liveliest Canadian journal of her day. I turn to page 354 of Volume I, where Maud tells how the great *Marcopolo*, once the world's fastest ship, came to grief. It was on July 25, 1883 — 116 years from tomorrow — and in her Cavendish schoolroom, all heard the sound of the vessel's doom.

> *Meanwhile, although we did not know it, a crowd of people were already gathered on the seashore, watching a magnificent sight — a sight I shall always regret not having seen — the*

> *sight of a large vessel coming straight on before the north gale*
> *with every stitch of canvas set. She grounded about 300 yards*
> *from the shore and as she struck the crew cut the rigging and the*
> *huge masts, one of them of iron, went over with the crash that*
> *we heard in the schoolroom a mile away.*

No lives were lost at the time. But locals came out to salvage its cargo of lumber, and another storm arose one night when they had unwisely stayed on the wreck. Three of them, "mad with fear," tried to reach shore in a boat that was soon swamped, and one was "drowned before our eyes."

The entire summer, Maud writes, "was a series of 'pictures' for me." The old ship's crew members, "being typical tars, painted our quiet village a glowing scarlet"; and when the men were paid in gold sovereigns at Maud's very home, their round mahogany table became heaped with unimaginable wealth. Maud keenly observed Captain Bull, who boarded there.

> *He was Norwegian, a delightful, gentlemanly old fellow who*
> *was idolized by his crew. He spoke English well but was apt to*
> *get mixed up in his prepositions and was as likely to thank you*
> *for your "kindness against" him as "to" him.*

Parallels with the *Empress of Ireland* come to mind. A revered ship sailing from Quebec. Disaster in the Gulf of St. Lawrence. Sudden death. Eager salvage attempts. A colourful captain.

The Leas first arrived on the *Valiant*, which gave passage to so many immigrants that a room in Charlottetown's Prince Edward Hotel is named after that vessel. Here I have the room opened for me by a beaming young employee, who points through the window at a pier for cruise ships.

I ask his opinion of the new Confederation Bridge, joining PEI to the mainland. "Not impressive," he answers in true Island style, the smile fading. "Twenty years from now, it'll be Long Island." This outlook would make Saint John, or perhaps Moncton, into a kind of Manhattan.

In 1897 my grandfather came to Fredericton, New Brunswick, his 19th Army appointment. On my return home in late afternoon I ask a ruddy-faced man where the citadel might be. This is Billy, a retired railroader, who knows the Army well. Once he played fiddle in the Army's basement — for a *dance*, I am amazed to learn.

You mean people dancing, holding one another to music, in an Army hall? I ask. They certainly did.

Billy also fiddled for his Aunt Frances at her nursing home, when she was 96. "Play 'Over the Waves,' she said — I did, and she got up and danced a jig. I cried, there were tears coming down on my fiddle! Then I said, 'What if Uncle Harry knew you were doing that?' and she said, 'Well, he'd jump right out of the grave and dance one with me!'"

Maritimers: people such as my ancestors well knew. "Waltzes, jigs — I played a lot of hymns, too, and even an Army march," Billy continues. "The sergeant couldn't believe it: doing a march on the fiddle. 'God bless you,' he said, 'playing something for the Army.'"

The citadel remains downtown — Billy claims that he talked the captain into keeping the location so that seniors could continue to walk there — and, says he, the place is packed every Sunday. On the door is a schedule of open-air services held in a riverside park.

Fredericton was one of my grandfather's last postings as an officer; his first had been further up the Saint John River, in Woodstock. That was in December 1885, even before the railway came here:

> *Ferried across one stream where the bridge had been broken down and drove around in a wagon to where there was another bridge gone, quite a lively time as we rode over the rough roads huddled together in a wagon. However arrived safe and well-saved in Woodstock in time to march along with Capt. Scott had good meeting one soul all glory to God. Hallelujah.*

Tonight in Woodstock's commodious new corps, the gym holds an Alcoholics Anonymous meeting. In the hall, leafing through the Army songbook, I remember a passage in David's diary about this corps in 1885: "Christmas Day and my first effort to sing a solo. Made a botch of it (all for Jesus)."

Salvationists, who value spontaneity, view the traditional seminary as a deadener of inspiration. There, one could dwell on minutiae for years while outside, the "weeping and wailing and gnashing of teeth" went unheard. Army theology amounted to little more than: humanity fell with Adam, but may connect with God's love again through Jesus.

Officers often faced a problem much harder than defining the nature of God: mob violence. "Jubilee large crowd, good time. Pretty rough outside, I got covered with flour and mud," David wrote at this time; for the *War Cry* he gave a report underlining the raw fury of local opposition:

> *On Thursday we had to take the open air, and the Devil had his brigade to the front. Eggs, potatoes, stones and cordwood came in all directions, but the Lord looked after us, and after having a good open air we marched off home escorted by the Devil's dupes.*

The Army's Greetings (1890).

At the same time, many were being "saved." In Springhill, Nova Scotia, one of David's colleagues said that the Army was "smashing the place up" by garnering over 250 conversions. New soldiers were kept busy with Army activities — playing in the band, rattling a tambourine, bearing flags, selling the *War Cry* in pubs, doing knee drill (prayer sessions) — yet still had animal spirits to burn off, as Cadet Cole relates:

The army is getting along nicely here the soldiers seem to be good but Oh they are fairly crazy after the girls and the girls are not much better. It is very hard fighting to get them to stop it but we are believing for some grand times here. They are very good hearted people but it is the same as other places there is lots of devilment going on. . . .

Novelist David Adams Richards, writing about the New Brunswick milieu a century later, presents a relativist ethos: "Everything is right and everything is wrong. It all depends on who's doing it when."

My grandfather was all for scourging inbred sin, but Ralphie Pillar in *Nights Below Station Street* sees only fate: "An object falls, it has no idea where it will land, but at every moment of its descent it is exactly where it is supposed to be."

Salvationists had the benefit, one might say, of viewing life as a conflict — not only on earthly battlefields but within the soul. An internal struggle faced by David, presumably over some barely avoided sin, is implied in an entry for March 6: "Praise God got a glimpse of Hell, God showed me what I am saved from."

Meanwhile, a friend back in Saint John kept David informed about corps activities, including an Army rite typical of that rough-and-tumble era: the "Hallelujah wedding":

Well, in the meeting there was a great uproar. The boys on the right hand side of the hall were as full of fun as ever and don't you forget they gave them a great cheering and stamping. When the marriage was over with and the persons went to sign the document, Capt. Hudson screams out, "Now Bob, do your duty!" and thereby was another uproar.

Anguish one moment, excitement the next. "Off to Saint John with party of soldiers to celebrate our first anniversary in Maritime Provinces," David writes for May 24, 1886. "Arrive safe, have banquet, grand march, large crowd in Roller Rink." Great times in New Brunswick!

FREE AND EASY

Rev. Dr. Hall said he did not believe there was any religion about the Salvation Army. In Kingston sacred things were turned into a jest. The barracks were nightly turned into a dancing hall, where they held what are called free-and-easy meetings. One soldier would get up with his head near the ceiling and remark that he was never so near God before, and then they would all laugh. He had attended two meetings, and at neither had the Bible been produced. He said the whole thing was a farce. It was an institution of the devil.
Christian Guardian, 1884.

DRIVING TO ONTARIO, I have dinner at Frankie Pesto's Restaurant in Kingston. It occupies the former Grand Trunk rail station, with well-carved stones masked by bogus grapevines. Wine bottles are festively hooped together in sculptures on the walls.

Ordering a pasta, I indulge also in a bottle of beer. For my clan until recently, to imbibe intoxicants would have been seen as a step toward hellfire. Yet I am confident that a spiritous glass may often do more good than harm — except for those who end up going to AA.

In 1889, at the end of David's Kingston posting as corps captain, he was carried to this station on comrades' shoulders, before setting out to his next command at Belleville. It had been an eventful stay.

Earlier the town's sober Christians had been mightily irked by the Army's unorthodoxy, as when "India Rubber Bill" Cooper gave sermons while balanced on his head, and spun cartwheels during Army parades. The Congregational Church's Dr. Hall judged Salvationism as "antagonistic" to the true Church of God.

Although Salvationists were forbidden to stop at any corner for meetings, they saw this as advice rather than the law, and felt secure doing open-air services. After all, no Army officer in Canada was ever convicted for obstructing the streets — until this happened to David in 1888.

On October 18 before the customary Thursday-night march,

David prayed for the Lord's help and then led his soldiers forth on Ontario Street. Before the O.K. House at Brock Street they paused, among bystanders who seemed neglectful of their souls. "I was constrained for conscience sake," David later wrote, "to stop with the intention of telling them of Jesus."

As the Salvationists sang "My home is in heaven," Police Sergeant Nesbitt came and asked them to leave. This was in response to a plea from hotelkeeper Owen Kennedy, irate over what he called "hollering and whooping" before his premises. David refused to budge, as no Salvationist was standing on the walk; Nesbitt took him and two comrades to the town jail and locked them up.

In 1888 the Salvationists engaged a lawyer, J. McIntyre. Brought next day before Police Magistrate Duff, they were charged with disorderly conduct, but dismissed when McIntyre showed that no case against them existed. On Saturday, however, a summons for foot-passenger obstruction was served against the three. "Not guilty," pleaded the prisoners in court before a large audience.

Kennedy went on to tell how he had taken the easiest course, simply to clear Army members away, because "they were not fit to be baptised yet." David took the stand to deny that obstructing the streets, or troubling anyone, was his wish. It was simply to preach, and invite other souls to their hall.

"I have nothing against the hotel keeper," said David, "except love." Magistrate Duff reaffirmed that the Army had no right to halt on the street, and had been so informed. McIntyre remarked that nothing had been done earlier when a brass band obstructed foot passage before the Opera House; how strange!

The Magistrate, said *The British Whig*, recalled that the court had "encouraged and assisted the Army in its work, and frequently those who had annoyed it in its worship had been punished." The Army should thus have been careful not to have erred on its part, by disturbing pedestrians. Judging the captain to be the chief offender, he fined David twenty dollars and costs.

When McIntyre appealed the decision, the case gained wide attention. "There is in all towns a feeling which permits the Army to enjoy privileges which other bodies would scarcely dare to take," said the *Brockville Recorder*, noting that members frequently "take up their stand upon some prominent part of the main thoroughfares, completely blocking the sidewalks with the crowd they gather about them, and forcing passers-by to wade ankle deep in the mud."

David told the *War Cry* that the appeal was set for December 11, adding, "Pray, my dear comrades, as I fear that my Christmas dinner will be neglected should we lose the case."

On December 6, the city solicitor consented to quash the conviction with costs to that date. "Captain Creighton, therefore, is completely exonerated," *The British Whig* declared, "and the Salvation Army scores a victory."

Today accordion tunes, as if from sunny Italy, are wafted through Frankie Pesto's. In 1888, there was Army music for David's farewell. "A large number of the soldiers followed in procession headed by the band," said the *War Cry*. "At the station they enjoyed themselves by singing hymns."

I visualize them as in a luminous 1883 photo portraying the Canadian Territory's first group of officers: young, intense, affectionate. And engaging. Abby Thompson, at lower right, became so well-known that a cleansing product was named after her: Abby Soap.

Most are women. But they have a male American commander, Major Thomas Moore, the full-bearded man sitting below "Happy Bill."

There was also a "Happy Will" McAdam who wrote letters to David. "My soul is fat and healthy, living on the bread & water of life from Heaven," he said in one of them. At Port Perry when toughs attacked the captain, Happy Will led a brave counterattack: "we pitched into them and piled them on top of the seats and made them gag and they begged off." Yet a Franciscan side to McAdam's nature comes out in a later message from Lindsay:

> *I love to talk to Jesus and I believe he loves to talk to me. As I go along the road and hear the little birds sing they seem to praise God and the flowers of the field it seems as though I can see God in it.*

Among the Army's friends in Kingston was Agnes Machar, the poetry-writing daughter of Queen's University's eminent principal, John Machar. Her *Red Cross Knights of the Salvation Army*, written in 1883, lauds the custom of giving testimony — the "red-hot shot," in Army phraseology — to declare changes wrought by God's love in everyday life. Courage is shown, she says, in giving voice before others: "and they speak with a simplicity, directness, and force which evidently come from the heart, and consequently go to the heart."

In Machar's account, we visualize the kind of "free-and-easy" service David must have led here in Kingston:

> *As each soldier finished his "testimony," it is usual for the captain to strike in with an appropriate verse of a hymn in which all join, sometimes repeating a chorus over eight or ten times, just as the impulse directs, while one or two stand waiting to speak until the hymn is finished. There is no routine and, within certain limits, variations are constantly occurring, so that at least there is no fear of monotony.*

As shadows lengthen I continue to Tweed, where the amazing Lottie Lowry became a Salvationist. Before she married Charles Creighton, David's younger brother, Lottie had served the Army out west.

The girl at the variety store counter, asked where the Army corps stands today, puts on a big smile and exclaims, "Next to the fire station, a block over from the main drag!"

"Tweed Corps 1888 / 1988," says a sign on the citadel, from which Lottie set forth, at 21, for Manitoba. "Men were everywhere and girls were nowhere," she wrote in a high-spirited memoir, "and yet, in spite of the wickedness and wildness of those surroundings, the Salvation Army lassie was treated with profound respect, and was an influence for good over the men with whom she came in contact."

Returning from outdoor worship on the bald prairie near Brandon, she and her comrades took refuge from storm in an empty house where lightning flashes served to locate "three treasures — one match, an old tin can, and some splinters of wood." Dexterously building a fire, they kept it going until the storm ended at daybreak and they continued homeward.

"A Few Words of Testimony," an 1894 *War Cry* article in Lottie's characteristically buoyant style, told about her work as the Army's leader in Winnipeg:

> *Our Camp Meetings were indescribable heavenly-times! I positively got the glory in my feet. I DID dance! This caused a sensation, but others followed until the whole platform, with few exceptions, were there as well.*

First officers'
council in
Canada, 1882.
(George Scott
Railton Heritage
Centre)

Lottie served as captain also in Vancouver, where longshoremen would naughtily show up at the penitent form merely to win bets, Lottie held a Hallelujah-wedding fundraiser for the struggling corps at Moose Jaw, Saskatchewan: "Tickets were sold for 50 cents each and we had a packed house."

Family of Charles Wilfred Creighton, circa 1916, young Cyrus at left.

Lottie was "united for war" with Charles Wilfred Creighton in 1896. They and daughters Muriel and Della are seen here with Cyrus, adopted after the *Empress* disaster.

This family also embraced my father. "Cyrus Wilfred" was the name he gave to my brother ("Fred" for short). Here, in a genuine sense, are my adoptive grandparents.

In the 1890s, the Army expanded its social services. The need for monetary support created a wish not to offend other churches — and, concurrently, meant the abandonment of many corps as evangelism receded.

Charles Creighton rose in the hierarchy, becoming Territorial Young People's Secretary for Canada. Then suddenly in 1909 he gave up officership — on learning that Thomas Coombs, the commissioner, coveted a Toronto mansion as his own retirement home. At this fractious moment Coombs also left the work, and the Army itself.

Idealism, perhaps, motivated Charles and Lottie's abrupt descent from the top Army circles. They moved to Calgary, where he sold shoes. The irony is that they now lacked funds to book passage on the *Empress of Ireland* — and thus survived to become second parents for young Cyrus.

Tweed and the Land O' Lakes, a lengthy tourist guide given out here, has much to say about Stoco Lake on the town's perimeter.

I am curious about a snapshot taken at the "U-GO-I-GO resort" on that lake, showing two lovely Creighton women. One is Muriel, Lottie's daughter. The other is Edith, with long hair that was then auburn like Bertha's and also Will's.

I show the photo to a number of elderly townspeople, none of whom can remember a resort of that name, and finally drive around Stoco Lake, managing to identify its probable location on what is now private land.

We see Edith during early adulthood — perhaps in 1914, when admiring comments appeared in her diary about sunny Guido Whatmore, who had an engaging smile. He perished on the *Empress* after giving his lifebelt to a distraught woman, said the *Telegram*; he "tried to assure her that all would be saved, but the words stuck in his throat, and she could see that he expected the worst."

As for Muriel, she was simply the kindest of all my aunts — and so gifted that she became secretary to Evangeline Booth during her term as the US Commander. Evangeline, who did not marry, was then in her sixties — still handsome, still keen about riding horses. While the two lived together, Eva would often conceive a new song in the small hours and ask Muriel to transcribe the melody. Finally Muriel suffered a nervous breakdown, under the pressure of work and these irregular hours.

Muriel and Edith Creighton, circa 1914.

UNITED FOR WAR

History seems a gentle avocation, orderly and consoling, until you get further into it. Then you see the shambles, the prodigal, dizzying, discouraging confusion. Just here, just on this one patch of the earth's surface where things have not been piling up for very long; so what does that say about the rest?

Alice Munro, "Names"

And the peace of God, which passeth all understanding, shall keep your hearts and minds through Christ Jesus.

Philippians 4:7

SOUTHWESTERN ONTARIO, OR "SOUWESTO," now shapes itself in our imagination largely through the writings of James Reaney, Alice Munro, Daniel David Moses. Fiction presents a complex world where human meaning is often elusive, while religion gives the grand and calming simplifications of faith.

Letters sent to David by Souwesto friends provide some idea of the Salvationists' late-nineteenth-century outlook. Many were from carriage-painter Walter Scott of Guelph, whose flowing script appears on stationary showing a bearded soldier with tambourine and cornet before a globe inscribed "THE WORLD FOR GOD."

On a late-July Sunday morning I visit this agricultural heartland, where David served from 1886 to 1893. His first Ontario posting was at Guelph, from which Scott later sent reports of corps occurrences — as when the "fountain" of Christ's blood gave redemptive power to a woman reclaimed from sin:

She had just came out of jail, after serving 21 days for keeping a disorderly house . . . and we got her in the fountain, and got her washed and properly converted, glory be to God, and we have had her in the marches and on the platform ever since, Hallelujah for such a setback to the devil and our policemen here.

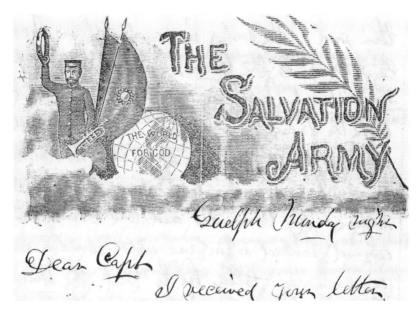

Letter from Walter Scott.

Scott, using the rich Biblical phraseology then natural to many believers, built metaphor on metaphor in messages of visceral triumph:

> *I feel that I could shake hands with death as with an old familiar friend, lift the veil of eternity, walk up to the Throne, and shout Hallelujah, Salvation to our God forever and ever. Glory be to God. But I am not going to die yet, God wants me to clout the devil a while longer, and when I cannot get my hands into his wool, then I will push my teeth and boots into him.*

Scott grew disheartened by a dearth of jobs, however, and confessed to reaping in his body "the effects of an illspent life." Yet always he signed off with a distinctive flourish: "Yours truly in the Harness" or "Yours truly in the War against Sin and the Devil" or "A Blood and Fire Soldier on my happy way to Heaven."

Scott later found work in nearby Fergus, and we are indebted to him for describing the street-corner meeting — a rite to which David's other correspondents give only scant reference:

> *I march the streets here alone with the lasses, and if we can get a crowd together in the open air, the Captain and I will lather into them, while the little Lieut. will go around them for a*

collection, and then we march back to the Barracks and thank
God for the victory in our souls. Thank God for a stand-up-to-
the-devil salvation. The people here don't know what to make of
me, and when I walk down street they will give me the whole of
the sidewalk to myself.

At St. Thomas in 1888, David demonstrated what a corps historian later called a "flair for showmanship" — torchlight processions were a big success — along with his usual concern for sinners. When an alcoholic man staggered into one open-air meeting and collapsed, David gained a conversion after sobering him up with black coffee:

During the chorus singing that opened Knee Drill, this haggard
looking drunkard began to weep. Suddenly, he jumped up and
ran to the Mercy Seat. There he threw himself "at the foot of the
cross," crying out for forgiveness.

"The St. Thomas saints are thumping the devil right hard," said David in the *War Cry*. "Our soldiers are going in for more holiness." The American evangelist Phoebe Palmer had told of a holiness achieved through surrender, Jesus being a kind of altar on whom any gift would be consecrated. Submissiveness, clearly, was central to the Army holiness experience.

David told how a St. Thomas woman held back from donning the Army uniform after conversion, fearing ridicule. To wear the severe "Hallelujah bonnet," designed as armour against hurled beer bottles and urine pots, meant a sacrifice of beauty. But she finally opted for the uniform after deciding "to put God's will in first place in her life."

I continue to Ingersoll, where Evangeline Booth once headed a fancy-dress Salvationist bicycle parade along the streets. That was shortly before she led Army officers into the Klondike, where miners would deposit gold dust in the collection plates. She became a key role-model for woman evangelists — notably, one later known as Sister Aimee Semple McPherson.

The Ingersoll corps, which still occupies its original site, was scandalized in early years over an "arrangement" made by fifteen-

Evangeline Booth, circa 1890.

year-old Minnie Peart. Having served as a nurse to the dying wife of a vigorous fifty-year-old farmer, she then married him — the two crossing into the US to do so, and giving their ages as 42 and 22. This occurred when David Creighton held the captain's rank at nearby Woodstock.

The couple's only child was a girl who also married in her teens and was destined, as Sister Aimee, to become the era's pre-eminent gospel shouter. She staged bizarre "Foursquare Gospel" epics to brass-band accompaniment in her vast Los Angeles temple, where Minnie handled the finances. Dressed as a policeman, Sister once entered the platform on a motorcycle, shouting, "Stop! You're speeding to ruin!"

Aimee famously vanished from a Pacific-coast beach only to appear in the Arizona desert with a claim that she had been kidnapped. The temple's handsome radioman disappeared at about the same time. And shortly the two, along with Minnie, were held for trial on conspiracy charges; after "a certain person of influence" was bought off for $6,000, they won a dismissal.

My family, living in California at the time of these indiscretions, gave Sister little regard. A Christian evangelist, yes, but not our kind of person. Too extreme, not serious enough, a little crazy.

Such characters figure in Alice Munro's fiction as "grotesques." She admired how Maud Montgomery used them as "conventions of what an entertaining novel should be." They reveal a kind of social decay visible in Munro's own part of Souwesto, the town of

Wingham. "The part of the country I live in is absolutely Gothic," she told an interviewer. "You can't get it all down."

One of her stories, "The Time of Death," describes a singer known as the Little Sweetheart of Maitland Valley. Sister Aimee always comes to mind when I read how this talented and prematurely grown-up youngster, Patricia Parry, accidentally scalds a mentally retarded child to death. There is a reference to the Army:

> *And the girl from the Salvation Army would say, in her gentle unchanging voice, You must forgive her, Mrs. Parry, she is only a child. Sometimes the Salvation Army girl would say: It is God's will, we do not understand.*

"The Time of Death" caused offence to some who saw it as the fictionalizing of an incident that actually occurred in Wingham. "We have been repeatedly made the butt of sour and cruel introspection on the part of the gifted author," said the local weekly, intensifying outrage that produced death threats to Munro.

For *Books in Canada* I once wrote an article about Munro's fiction, not realizing then how much I was trying to resolve. Merely in the way our world looks, she says, "there's this kind of magic." She says, "This ordinary life is sufficient, everything here touchable and mysterious."

Is transcendence to be awaited in the beyond, or found and in our own lives? I admire Munro's delight in the mind's grasp of reality: "exploring the pattern of it, feeling all those lives, and streets, and hidden rooms and histories, coming to light, seeing all the ceremonies and attitudes and memories in your power."

Writing, said Munro, is "a sort of wooing of distant parts of myself." Not decision-making but human possibility. Not divine revelation but personal statement. And yet, "the hope of accuracy we bring to such tasks is crazy, heartbreaking."

At Woodstock in 1997, Salvationists forsook their downtown location for a big new one near the 401 highway, between a Kelsey's and a Super-8 Motel. "God bless you," says the elderly greeter, much impressed to learn that my grandfather once served here. He was on the *Empress*, I add. "On the *Empress*! Really!"

A centennial booklet is soon in my hands, showing that David took command here on July 14, 1887. He is listed between a Captain

Helena and a Captain Etta, the only male among Woodstock's first eight appointees. Following in 1891 was Captain Gideon Miller, who designed the *Empress* memorial.

The new corps is called a Salvation Army *church*. Impossible, an oxymoron! Basic strategy overturned! Church fripperies — stained glass, stuffy organ tunes — were seen by William Booth as offputting to down-and-outs, who could relax in plain Army halls. Even taverns were put to use as citadels during his day: come as you are, no spit-and-polish, enjoy the fun.

Eleven a.m.: the band files in from their special room. Not like the forties at East Toronto corps, when it would arrive from open-air sessions raising a brass-and-drum tumult meant to lure bystanders into our hall. Such tactics today, down at the 401 intersection, might yield more fatalities than conversions.

"Well good morning, everyone!" booms the captain as things get underway. *Good morning!* we reply, then join in singing, "This-is-the-day, this-is-the-day that the Lord hath made!" That driving Army beat: we clap this one out, some doing tricky syncopations.

Big smiles attend "free-and-easy" worship such as William Booth would have endorsed.

"You all sat down — guess what, I'm going to ask you to stand and sing again!" cries the captain. Beethoven's Ninth is the basis for our next song, such adaptation having been approved by Booth ("Why should the devil have all the good tunes?").

Joyful, joyful we adore Thee, pretty good stick work by the drummer. "We have so much to be joyful for, don't we?" says the officer, "lining out" the third verse:

> *Teach us how to love each other,*
> *Lift us to the joy above.*

Musical selections: the songsters, then the band. Announcements: self-denial fund. Bible passage: *Philippians*. Pre-Message prayer: "We need to know what your spirit says to us, Lord."

And Message: Spiritual joy, how bitterness can ruin it. "Look at verse 19 . . . heavenly joy . . . verse 22 . . . are you cursed with bitterness? . . . verse 25 tells us. . . ."

I writhe in boredom. This Message lacks the punch of one heard recently at Vancouver's needle-park Harbourlight corps, which likened Christ's wounds to those of addicts.

"Can you begin to live a life of Christian joy?" we are asked. Too abstract. "Are you cursed with bitterness — maybe toward friends who got a promotion, and passed you by?" Ho-hum.

A chorus begins on the organ; so the Appeal must be next. Sins to be pondered, lives changed — although the likelihood of anyone "coming forward" now seems remote. "Perhaps there are some who have been caught up in bitterness . . . perhaps you need to come this morning . . . come and kneel at this place of prayer."

Softly we sing the chorus, meant to create a mood that would draw penitents to the mercy seat.

> *He knows, He knows*
> *The storms that would my way oppose*
> *He knows, he knows*
> *And tempers every wind that blows.*

Now here is tinder to ignite the Holy Spirit. *He knows, he knows*: a high note and a higher one, followed by *the storms* in low register, beautifully melodious. Quadruple rhyme. And metaphor: celestial heft above the turmoil of human realms.

While I analyze the tune, a woman advances to the mercy seat. Then another. Abruptly, an athletic-looking youth. And two bandsmen. There was something in the Message after all.

Soldiers now come forward to kneel alongside those who have made the move, offering counsel. One reaches her arm across in a light embrace.

Back in 1887 the soldiers here were more demonstrative, as a letter to David shows: "One old lady began to cry for mercy, and ere long followed by her husband made her way to the penitent form where they wept and confessed their sins."

The chorus continues on the organ: *he knows* loftily reassuring, *the storms* implying distress. It is one thing to savour Christian piety by hearing a Bach CD, and quite another to be in the midst of those for whom the music means everything. I am fascinated by the tears of empathy splashing down on my song book.

"Sing that song again," the captain requests, continuing his prayer. "We live by our own agendas, Lord, but gaining joy means letting You have control." Eventually only one woman remains at the mercy seat, a soldier gesticulating beside her. Their heads occasionally bob, as if at the acknowledgment of some truth.

Holiness is within her reach. Holiness as a victory over bitterness or whatever moral flaw must be quelled. Holiness as a "second blessing" following conversion: for Salvationists, here is the culmination of all spiritual effort.

"Sing the chorus again, that will be our benediction," we are told, and at its close the congregation begins to leave. The tune continues, *pianissimo*, on the organ.

All is hushed, several worshippers remaining here in vigil for this penitent soul, until finally the two arise and then all depart, the organist building volume slightly at the end.

David Creighton the Army officer, the friend of immigrants, the devoted father of five, the leader tragically lost on the *Empress* — who was he? Someone who could smile at a dirty joke? A man capable of acting out of character? Omit any such details, some would say.

An anonymous letter received at Woodstock by my grandfather, then single and ruggedly handsome, gave advice about a certain Miss Moore: "Both you and the Lieut. make too much of her to suit outsiders, they know her better. Take heed from a friend that would not like the officers to be disgraced falsely." Special attention shown by the captain to any woman, of course, would be swiftly noted.

"I cannot get you out of my mind," a female admirer confessed in one note — which, like the other, remained in David's possession until death. "Perhaps you will think I am not very wise or going silly, well it doesn't matter very much as you don't know me."

Woodstock truly did become the scene of scandal, extra-marital sinning, not long after his departure — as shown by another letter: "You will be sorry to learn that at last, Ex-Lieutenant Greenwood and Mrs. Garnett have left for the States." It continues in a Biblical vein: "Poor Ben (Samson over again) his hair was taken long ago . . . his strength was gone and the Philistines got him."

We may surmise that David steered clear of iniquity at Woodstock, having set his heart on auburn-haired Bertha Jane Dixon, the corps sergeant-major. She had just turned 18 — born on Valentines Day, 1869 — and he was 23.

David once hoped that both she and her mother, Theresa, might

Bertha Creighton, circa 1890.

attend one of the summer's camp meetings in Guelph. "The spirit truly is willing but the flesh is weak," Theresa replied, complaining that the fatigue would be too much for her. "The men are busy and Bertha will not be going as I need her at home. It is very kind for you to offer to find us a place to stay."

Bertha, who often lent protection to women lieutenants by staying over at their residence, soon contemplated officership for herself. Theresa speculated on whether God would call Bertha: "I am thankful I live where I can say 'Thy will be done.' But as you say, it is well to know when it is His voice." The Army offered women equal preaching opportunity, a wonder in that day.

Bertha Dixon, finding "divine favour" much as David had, became an Army officer in 1890. She rose to the rank of lieutenant while serving at Drayton, Strathroy, and Tillsonburg.

Officers would marry within the ranks, to maximize their soul-saving efforts, and the phrase *united for war* was often seen beneath *War Cry* photos of Army couples soon to be married. For David and Bertha, such a union would be ideal.

Who was my grandmother? Only a few details emerge from the correspondence in which she is mentioned, mainly postcards showing the family's mutual devotion. "Dear Mother: Auntie wants me to stay a few days. Your loving son W.H. Creighton." To Master Willie, Bertha later wrote a boys'-level message from St. Catharines: "There are lots of boats passing — one was called the 'Panther.'"

Also I have a few memories of her that Will shared with me. Whenever I felt a mood of resentment, he would repeat a phrase used by Bertha: "Don't cut off your nose to spite your face." I can imagine its application to rancorous goings-on within an Army citadel, or her own large family.

Only recently coming to light are several items apparently found in my grandfather's desk after his demise: a dozen 1914 railway passes, notes regarding his emigration-secretary tasks, letters stating a wish for advancement. "Many things have suggested themselves to me," muses David the idea-man, "which I believe would obtain better results if once in operation."

Here is my grandfather near the end of a life devoted to the Army cause, served largely in citadel postings of short duration. It was demanding toil. A letter regarding Bertha sent to David Rees — in 1913, a year before all three would drown — earns a reply by the commissioner in his typically old-world style of address:

My brother Fred is amused by the subtexts here. "This letter says, 'I can be all things to all people,'" he remarks. "And here's our grandmother looking for a little leisure time." After the challenges of corps officership, Bertha cherishes a life enjoyed *behind the scene*.

Letter from
Commissioner
Rees, 1913.

My dear Major,-

re Mrs. Creighton.

I have your letter and will keep the matter well before me. I endorse to the very full all you say about your beloved wife's willingness to toil on behind the scene. I do think that some of our dear wives set to us men an example that ought to bring great inspiration and blessing to our hearts. Be assured that I will do my utmost in this matter.

God bless you.

Believe me,

Yours in faithful affection,

David M. Rees
Commissioner.

The note also points to what Fred calls the Army's "matriarchal" underpinnings. Current Salvationist thinking emphasizes the role initially played by the Founder's wife, Catherine. "She is thought to be the real brains behind it," he notes, "with William Booth only her puppet."

Catherine Booth's conversion trials, her search for "new light," are part of the Army's lore: "I used to pace my room till two o'clock in the morning, and when, utterly exhausted, I lay down at length to sleep, I would place my Bible and hymn-book under my pillow, praying that I might wake up with the assurance of salvation."

David and Bertha were married at Woodstock on October 20, 1892. A *War Cry* correspondent gave an account of their nuptials in the light-hearted Salvationist style: "I arrived just before 9 a.m., and, walking down the street, met Captain Creighton, so my mind was at rest as to whether he had forgotten the day or date."

Army friends arrived from all around. "From 6 to 7:30 quite a number took in the supper, and got ready for a good meeting." They enjoyed a march led by the local Army band, then "went in for a good time."

Army weddings often featured an old cannon, for making joyful noise unto the Lord. On this occasion, rousing testimonies to happy union with Christ were given before ceremonies began:

The Army service was read, the parties

Promised to be Faithful

to God and the Army and to each other; the knot was tied, which I trust neither of these comrades will ever regret, but that many souls, and the kingdom of God generally, will have cause to praise God for. God bless them both.

David and Bertha
Creighton, 1892.

107

TORONTO IS IN TEARS;
CANADA MOURNS

Oh, bitter and sad was the blow to the Army!
Its leaders and bandsmen snatched rudely away;
But faith rallied quickly, and girded its weapons,
And eyes, dimmed with tears, turned away to the fray.
Herbert Wood, "The Empress"

THE MAIN HALL OF Toronto's Union Station, barrel-vaulted like ancient Roman baths, is carved with the names of Canadian cities: *FORT-WILLIAM REGINA MOOSE JAW CALGARY VANCOUVER.*

In 1912, when David Creighton made one of his trips accompanying New Canadians to locations across the land, Edith ("Tootsie" to her adoring father) went along. "We are in Montreal," she said. "We are leaving for Que at 1:30 today." That is, at the Quebec City docks David would first meet immigrants newly arrived on the CPR's Atlantic Service.

Four days later he wrote, "We are now past Brandon and have had a good sight of the wheat fields and they are tremendous in size."

Long gone is the earlier depot that was a departure-point for them — and, two years later, for Salvationists travelling to meet the *Empress of Ireland.* Its only remaining fragment, westward in the SkyWalk where the elevated walkway crosses York, is a stone bearing the words CANADIAN NATIONAL RAILWAY.

Photos hanging nearby portray my grandparents' world. "Full steam ahead, circa 1907": three fuming engines burnished by the sun. "Delivery truck — catching a ride": muddy track, horse, wagon with a grinning boy at the back. "Morning rush hour circa 1911": workmen in caps and worn suits cross the cinder-strewn tracks.

In a railway-nostalgia shop I request items about the CPR's Atlantic Service. "Forgotten," says the sales clerk. "Nothing was saved." Yet after rummaging about, he exclaims, "Oh, I've got something for you, very rare!"

For seven dollars I acquire an officer's button bearing the Atlantic Service's checkerboard flag. "Here's something else you might like,"

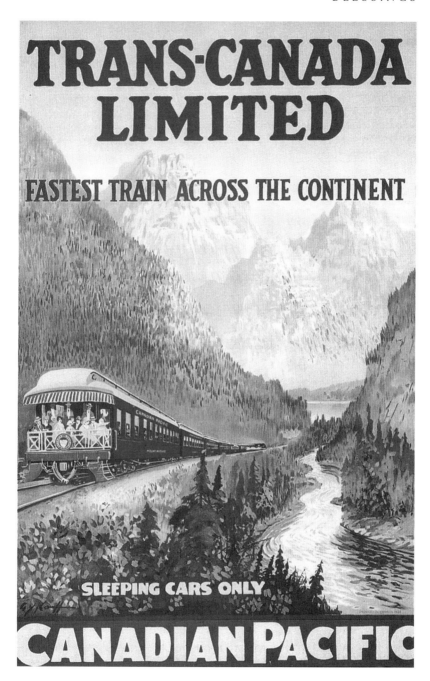

Canadian Pacific poster, 1924.
(Canadian Pacific Limited)

Canadian
Pacific
baggage tag.

Chris adds. An Atlantic Service baggage sticker, with space for "sailing date" and "port of landing," is mine for $3.50.

Looming now is the 11:30 departure of a train announced on the PA: "OSHAWA — BELLE-VILLE — KING-STON — BROCK-VILLE — CORN-WALL — DOR-VAL — AND — MONTREAL."

In 1914 Congress delegates bound for their Atlantic Service liner were scheduled for departure just before midnight. But to the joy of those saying goodbye, the train remained still for almost an hour.

A derailing caused the delay. "That certainly was something unusual," wrote *War Cry* sub-editor Edward Dodd, London-bound with his wife, "but unusual things are ever occurring in the Army."

So the farewells continued. "The rafters of the station rang with well-known Army choruses," Dodd added; these were "taken up by their fortunate comrades in the long sleeper cars." Many Salvationists had come from elsewhere in Ontario, with drum and tambourine, for the big send-off.

Some had known the Army's earliest days. The years of struggle, persecution, youthful triumph.

Today at Gate 9, goodbyes are given again to Quebec-bound passengers: "See you later! . . . Have fun, guys! . . . Okay, bye-bye, okay!" A woman rushes into the souvenir shop to buy a pair of teddybear Mounties — "For my grandchildren," she says — before climbing the steps to her train.

All the Creighton children must have been on hand to see their parents off, although no recollections of that night have been preserved.

"Little groups of Salvationists were to be seen at the entrances to the coaches," Dodd wrote in 1914, "right until the train started." The singing continued — "No, never alone," "Over the sea" — and finally,

> *The Maple Leaf forever;*
> *God bless our Army round the world,*
> *And keep us true forever.*

At 12:25 a.m. the train began to move. Alongside ran the delegates' loved ones, waving handkerchiefs and crying out their good wishes.

Around five on the morning of May 29, 1914, Staff Captain William Arnold heard his house phone ringing. It was the editor of the Toronto *Globe*, with a message that communicated, the *War Cry* later said, "an awful sense of horror."

A press despatch had come to the *Globe* from Rimouski at 3:08 a.m., but gave only meagre details. Arnold phoned three other officers and all were soon at the Army's downtown headquarters, the Temple, calling to inform relatives that something had happened to the *Empress*. He instructed them to be "as hopeful as possible that their loved ones had been rescued."

Letterhead showing Salvation Army Temple, circa 1910.

A multitude gathered outside, rushing to scan each bulletin posted by the entrance. *All are safe,* came a message at eleven o'clock, stirring the crowd to raise a cheer and shout, "Thank God!" Several optimistically returned to work.

But the dread continued. Then a wire finally came to verify the worst fears. Pathetic sobbing began, and many suffered total collapse. This was the message:

May 29, 1914

LATEST REPORT RECEIVED — 1:30 *p.m.*

No reliable authority can be found to confirm the message previously sent — that all are safe.

According to information which has reached Montreal from Rimouski — The Vessel was struck amid-ships, and that she began to sink immediately. The water rushed in so fast that she tipped over on her side.

This is the story from one of those who were in a Life Boat. All were in Bed at the time of the disaster. Great confusion getting the Life Boats out.

The latest information is — Over 900 lost. This is from Rimouski.

Night arrived here as "a black mass of humanity surged around the Temple, anxiously awaiting a promised telegram confirming the list of survivors." At last it came: no more than twenty names, those of Major and Mrs. Creighton not among them.

"At one point it was on record that the body of D.L. Creighton, second in command of the Salvation Army Immigration Department, was on its way to the city, along with the bodies of Adjutant Harry Green and Captain Guido Whatmore," said a June 2 edition of the *Mail and Empire*, "but later all three names were erased from the list."

One man reading the survivors' list gasped, "Is that all!" and leaned against the door, said the *Star*. "A bonnetted Army lass patted his arm to comfort him, and ended by burying her face on his shoulder and sobbing unrestrainedly."

A girl reading the bulletin board "stumbled over the steps of the entrance, sobbing bitterly," the *Globe* reported. She was "borne unconscious upstairs" and on awakening "moaned for her lost brothers in a heartrending manner."

Stories told later about the sinking *Empress* were appallingly vivid. More and more terrible the passengers' plight appeared. It had been a Darwinian fight for survival. And as the brief list of the identified dead took firm shape, it became clear that many had been trapped within the *Empress*, and remained there still.

Colonel French now arrived from Chicago, said the US *War Cry*, "on a mission of visitation of the bereaved families." His report gives the first of only two known references to David and Bertha's offspring at this hour:

> We were also privileged to see Commissioner Rees' son, and the Creighton children. Conditions prevailing beggar description. Sorrow and grief prevail everywhere. The fortitude and resignation manifested make us conscious of the presence of God as a consoler in a very real sense. Toronto is in tears; Canada mourns.

The Temple was then located at 18 Albert Street, where a modernistic building later rose in its place. This was recently demolished, and its very address is gone, the roadway having been usurped by a new Eaton Centre entrance.

This morning, crews are at work on the exedra-style structure. "The old Salvation Army?" says a man pouring cement. "I used to hang out right here — leave Eaton Centre, and there's the Army on the right side of the street!"

Still opposite the Temple's site is the old City Hall, which provided background for a 1914 photo of the Staff Band. White Xs were drawn on the photo to show those who survived, nine out of the original thirty-nine. For only the strong survived, only the ones able to climb those backward-slanting stairs. Only the experienced swimmers. Only the young.

This morning I have brought along the Staff Band photo, to discover its setting. In the background are columns of heavy stone dividing four windows, and this site connects with the City Hall's east side, opposite the Duke of Richmond pub. But the surfaces do not match up.

A man happens to be doing repairs here now, and is able to explain this conundrum. "See that stone?" he says, pointing above. "It went in a

Territorial Staff Band before Toronto City Hall, 1914.
(George Scott Railton Heritage Centre)

year ago." Replacements are formed from rock dust that he moulds within a form; thus, many stones will show exactly the same pattern.

Therefore to connect site with memory now, to re-experience here the pain of 1914, mourners have only this section of reconstituted wall.

The anguish intensified again on May 30, when multitudes packed that older Union Station to await a train bearing the first party of *Empress* survivors. White badges of mourning were on the arms of Salvationists — not black, as the dead had gone to heaven. Yet here on earth it had come to this: only a few shaken survivors.

These were "enfeebled from grief and suffering," said the *Mail and Empire*, bearing witness to "one of the great sea tragedies of the age." Down they stepped from the train, those few Army survivors.

What could Salvationists be thinking now? The Canadian leadership had been decimated, dear friends lost, families broken up forever. Many had devoted their lives to a realization of their faith's ideals — what did God mean by taking their lives?

It was reported that "a small soprano voice, sounding peculiarly weak, commenced to sing 'Praise God from Whom all blessings flow.'" Blessings, for the benevolence and love shown by the Almighty. *Blessings*.

The hymn "Old Hundred" followed, everyone removing their hats in sympathy. The song was taken up by those all around, "and went swelling through the station."

Scenes of this kind, rail-station arrivals made by a paltry few *Empress* survivors, recurred in many parts of North America. Only three Vancouverites came back, of thirty or so who had sailed. A similar number left from Winnipeg; Second Class passenger James Lennon seems to have been the only one to reappear. From Hamilton also some thirty passengers set forth; the sole survivior was an L.W. Hunt, England-bound to practise dentistry.

Departing from Regina, never to be seen again, was a Mr. A.H. Death. Adam and Jacob Lubnjewsky set out from Montreal; only the latter rejoined their family. Mr. and Mrs. John Black of Ottawa, Second Class travellers, were rescued — but not their fellow-citizen Mrs. E. Seybold, in First Class. Hilda Walkky of Quebec City, among the fortunate few Third Class voyagers to be saved, was in the process of being deported.

Many Americans booked passage on the *Empress*, mostly in Third Class. At least two dozen left from Chicago; Anastazia Rogozin (one of three in her family) was among the few to return. Over thirty departed from Duluth, Minnesota; Paolo Morrelli and Domenico Pierpoli were the sole survivors. Of more than sixty Ford Motor workers who set out from Detroit, only Mitrofim Kolometz and Jan Korga and Foma Malaschcuk came back.

Passenger-rescue statistics for Third Class indicate a situation to which the phrase "Women and Children First" hardly applies:

Women: 17 of 169
Children: 1 of 102
Men: 115 of 446

Toronto was the hardest hit of the municipalities touched by this calamity. Its passenger toll exceeded all others, and the Army's headquarters were located here. Sea disaster now produced a large city's collective ritual response, such as had never attended the sinking of the *Titanic* or any other great liner.

On June 6 at the Mutual Street hockey arena, Salvationists held a lying-in-state of the sixteen retrieved bodies. "As Rachel of old mourned for her children and would not be comforted, so Toronto mourns for those who, a few brief days since, left them in all the strength and brightness of life," said the Sunday *World*, in Biblical terms then familiar to most readers. Salvationists, known for the simplicity of their lives, were now accorded "the sweet simplicity of true and deep sorrow."

A scruffy field and the Terrace Housing Co-op today occupy the arena's site. I visualize the sixteen caskets lying in the middle; at the north end, Army flags and Union Jacks flanking letters that formed the word *VICTORY*;and opposite, floral tributes banked around a large horizontal cross.

Empress funeral, Mutual Street Arena, June 7, 1914.
(George Scott Railton Heritage Centre)

"It was 88 Mutual Street," notes Berndt, a recent New Canadian from Bavaria. "It was right there." The arena was later modified into a roller-rink which, says a marker, once hosted the Glenn Miller Band and Frank Sinatra.

Berndt recalls bitter outcry by rollerskaters at the loss of this popular rink — their only Toronto venue — and he points eastward to where a replacement was to have risen, if promises made then had been kept. "Times change, nothing stays the same," he reflects, adding that in Bavaria, such an urban treasure would have been seen as "part of the city, part of history."

In 1914 a multitude of mourners entered through the Mutual Street doors. The crowd, four deep, by mid-morning stretched back along Dundas Street, down Dalhousie, and along Shuter. "Please keep moving," said the officer in charge. "There are thousands waiting in the street now."

At the centre, where a dirt path runs today, was the coffin of Mrs. Rees. Her husband's body, miraculously found a month later, would become the focal point for further rites.

"Contrary to the expectations of many, the caskets were open, disclosing to view the tenants lying cold in their last earthly sleep," said the *Star*. "Working men, leaving their teams outside, filed in with bared heads and quiet, roughened faces." A small white coffin holding the baby, Margaret Foord, was approached by a gaudily dressed girl; then, "both hands suddenly covered her face to blot out the memory of the small baby face kissed to death by the waters of the river."

"The *Empress* funeral was the largest in the history of Toronto," Gideon Miller wrote in his diary. "The Arena was crowded with people of all creeds and classes, and thousands outside." It began at 2:30 on Sunday afternoon, June 7.

A long-threatening storm broke during the first hymn, "Abide with Me," lending booms of thunder to music of the massed Army bands:

> *Abide with me! Fast falls the eventide;*
> *The darkness deepens; Lord, with me abide!*
> *When other helpers fail, and comforts flee,*
> *Help of the helpless, oh, abide with me!*

The prayers began. "Dignitaries of court and council bowed head with the great concourse of people who earn their bread in the humbler walks of life," said the Sunday *World*. "'Amens' were heard but infrequently until the voice of thankfulness that there was an eternal hope was raised. Then they came in hundreds."

The 46th Psalm was intoned — "like the bursting of a ray of sunshine through a cloud" — and more addresses followed, the *World* noting how each speaker's words "rang with an unusual sublimity."

Colonel French spoke of seeing Evangeline Booth in New York, just before leading an American contingent overseas on the *Olympic*.

Asked what he should say to her Canadian comrades, Eva replied, "Go and tell them my heart is bleeding."

Thomas Coombs rose to represent the bereaved, having lost both a daughter and son-in-law. Struggling initially to calm a trembling voice, he then lifted his message to triumphant heights.

"Visions have come to me," said Coombs, presenting a mental vista of the maimed and the fallen with hands stretched out. "What do they ask? What is their cry? What is the burden of their poor hearts? They want Salvation."

One supreme question hung in the air: what had happened to the Commissioner? He was the Canadian leader, and many wished to view him as a kind of Lord Nelson perishing aboard the *Victory*. Now, they awaited testimony that his death had been noble, Christlike.

Staff-Captain David McAmmond, "with tears in his eyes and a tremour in his voice," told of seeing Rees fight his way up the stairs: "Then I saw him go down below again; it seemed as though he was after some of his party."

Staff Bandsman Jim Johnson remembered him struggling like all the others to get upstairs: "Commissioner Rees and some others were just going along in front of me and I assisted them in getting up as well as I could, and eventually lost sight of them."

Another eyewitness was Ensign Ernest Pugmire, who had been rescued "cold and numb and hardly able to move." To the *War Cry* he said, "Commissioner Rees, his wife, and family stood at the railing. He was calm; he may not have known the worst." But in the Toronto *World*, Pugmire was more memorably quoted:

> *I saw Commissioner Rees, when he ran back to get his wife.*
> *Major Frank Morris tried hard to save him, for he carried him*
> *on his shoulders for as long as he could. Morris was a hero.*

This image connected with the summary of Salvationists response given in a British *War Cry* editorial on June 6, 1914: "disregard of self, composure, and readiness to help others." It added a portrait of sublime bravery:

> *Commissioner Rees' noble decision and resignation to the Divine*

will; and brave Frank Morris swimming in water just above the freezing point, with his Commissioner on his back until he was overcome by exhaustion.

General Bramwell Booth provided other flourishes from hearsay:

Dear Commissioner Rees stands on deck calming and helping the stricken people, refusing to leave his wife and daughters, and cries aloud as the vessel sinks, "My God, Thy will be done!"

But a jarring account by Morris in the Canadian *War Cry* told it otherwise. The conditions, he pointed out in explicit terms, did not permit heroics:

The darkness, explosions, undercurrents, the water alive with hundreds of human beings struggling for their lives, the final sinking of the ship, which dragged us down, down into those icy waters, and many other terrible experiences, made rescue of this kind beyond human power, and especially when one was in the water without support of any kind.

Now on Memorial Sunday, he said, "I am here to testify that my comrades knew how to live, and thanks be to God, they knew how to die." Tragedy was now seen as an emblem of Salvationism: readiness for death, surrender to divine providence, clear hope of meeting loved ones beyond. Army tradition was being reaffirmed in its essential purity.

Listeners keenly awaited Morris's account of those final moments with the commissioner. Not letting them down, he gave a new remembrance of Rees at the stairway, as many struggled to reach the deck: "When I told him in a whisper of what had happened, he nodded his head and said, 'Yes, God's will be done.'"

Outside were the funeral cars, draped with purple and crepe and each drawn by four black horses caparisoned also in black and purple. As the service ended, the task of removing caskets to these vans commenced.

In accompaniment, massed military bands now played an orchestral version of the searing Funeral March from Chopin's opus

Empress funeral.
(George Scott Railton Heritage Centre)

35 piano sonata. Readiness for war, long building in Europe and the colonies, found one of its last peacetime expressions as members of the local militia, in full regimentals, prepared to walk at the rear of a vast procession to Mount Pleasant Cemetery.

"SALVATION FLAGS WILL LEAD GREAT FUNERAL CORTEGE," said the *Star*.

"All colour-sergeants will meet at the corner of Shuter and Church Streets," it advised; on Dalhousie Street (which today meets Shuter amid vast car-park spaces) would be gathered "the flowers, the caskets on draped drays, and the mourners."

St. Michael's Catholic Cathedral and Metropolitan United Church flank Shuter Street nearby. The Salvation Army puts all of its artistic splendour into brass bands, and in 1914 over a dozen paraded in a funeral procession such as Toronto had never seen.

At 4:50 the marchers set out along Shuter, one section of Army massed bands going before and after the coffins. Other bands bracketed first the mourners and then soldiers from various corps and societies. "The Salvationists will march to the last resting place of their comrades and will not ride in any conveyances," said the *Star*.

Crowds along its route filled each sidewalk, balcony, and window;often they overspread roofs. Over 100,000 people lined the route, and most were moved above all to see those few survivors who had escaped death only a week before. *Toronto is in tears; Canada mourns.*

A decade later the Army's redemptive fervour would be downplayed in favour of "character building" — talk more acceptable to those giving money to the cause — but now its bold pioneering days were uppermost in the mind. "The quality of their work," said Toronto's Anglican bishop, "must stand as a challenge and example for others to imitate."

Gideon Miller gave a concise report of the march: "The funeral procession, first a cluster of the united flags about 25 in number. Thousands of people lined the street all the way up Yonge to the cemetery, all with hats off, many weeping. The service was heart-touching at the grave."

Empress funeral, Mount Pleasant Cemetery
(George Scott Railton Heritage Centre)

As the cortège entered Mount Pleasant Cemetery's gates, the bands lined up outside to play "Nearer My God to Thee." Graves had been arranged with a space in between for the monument yet to be placed there. A lengthy mound of earth from the graves was heaped with wreaths, making it resemble a bank of flowers.

A deeply solemn effect was created, said the *Mail and Empire*, by "the soft blue of the sky, the green trees on every side, and the calm of evening stealing over all." As the interments were about to begin, a soloist aptly sang,

> *Oh, now to God be crying,*
> *For time is quickly flying,*
> *In the grave you'll soon be lying,*
> *Ere the sun goes down.*

That evening a final Memorial Day service was held at Massey Hall. Someone writing for the Army's junior publication, the *Young Soldier*, here made the second known record of the Creighton offspring at this time. It suggests how heavily the *Empress's* shadow had fallen on them:

> *In the congregation were the children of Major and Mrs Creighton, in the care of three kindly-faced uncles of the children. Cyrus, about three years of age, happy in the arms of Uncle Cyrus, being too young to realize his loss. Arthur, aged eight, and Willie, Edith and Wilfred, all sorrowfully realizing they now were orphans.*

PART THREE

The Power of Myth

THE REAL END IS
THE JOURNEY

From Partisan Pictures I get a request to join the *Lost Liners* documentary crew in Rimouski, for participation in an *Empress* segment to be filmed there in early August. I phone up Mark Reynolds, also involved in the shoot, and he lets on that Robert Ballard will be there.

"But it'd be better not to preannounce it, we wouldn't want to have a flotilla of boats gathering around," he adds. "The profile of the thing is big, a full-blown documentary. Big dollars, spare no expense."

This is not my speed at all, but Mark lends reassurance. "Should be a nice day on the water for you," says he. "Bring along your Ballard books, get them signed."

I have been asked to provide original family photos as well as some things I might read on camera. Gathering these and some clothing in a briefcase, off I go on an Air Canada jet.

On board, I get out a letter from Bertha Creighton — the only one by her I've ever seen. And also the last, written to her children on the train to Quebec City.

"Help Edie by being kind to Cyrus," she says to Arthur from the beyond. And there below, running near Lake Ontario, is the very rail line on which she penned this.

The letter is newsy, affectionate, humorous. Bertha tells Wilfred about the Staff Band, which was managing the meals: "I was telling Papa I could take pointers from them against the time when I run a boarding house. Ha Ha."

To Cyrus she says, "We saw some little chickens, brown, just the size of sparrows. Mama is lonesome for her little boys — How nice it would be if Arthur could have come. He would enjoy it." The longest message is to Edith, four paragraphs of instructions.

Trouble in the seats opposite: one man berates another for overloading the luggage compartment so as to crumple his clothing bag. "Don't be rude," says the younger one and then, after a harsh rejoinder, "*You* know what I'm talking about!" Ugly.

For Bertha, there was the surface-travel benefit of togetherness, of new people entering all down the line. Crossing over into Quebec, she cites French expressions now being heard — *Merci beaucoup, Très bien, Oui oui* — and gives a lesson in this tongue she once learned: *"Voulez vous venir* — That is, Will you come?"

Brigadier Walker has the upper berth, Bertha notes. Adjutant Beckstead had been sitting with her. "Willard Potter is stepping around and Gracie Hannigan with her mother." Of all these, Grace alone would escape sudden death.

We descend toward Montreal — for Bertha, at its rail station, only a brief stop. "We are halting a few moments, Major Simco and others coming aboard."

This was Nettie Simco, who had stayed with Montreal friends. She had had a premonition, one that she must have retold on the train — a vision of corpses in procession, crossing over water.

Here I walk to the connector, to complete my own trip down the St. Lawrence. On our twin-prop Beechcraft the captain and co-pilot are in full view, twiddling levers and knobs all along our river path.

A water bottle and one ham sandwich make up our complimentary meal: I think of Charles Lindbergh, first to solo the Atlantic and doing so on six hastily packed sandwiches.

"Will soon be at Quebec," my grandmother writes. "We are ahead of the Regular so will get aboard first." I now glimpse Quebec City from above, through a cloud-rift: point of final departure.

To Willie she remarks, "I appreciate very much your kindness on that last evening. It was hard enough leaving you all behind." My father adored her; what he showed on this occasion might have been simply an extra tenderness, or care.

We have a stop at Baie-Comeau, its airstrip a postage stamp amid vast forest lands. The Beechcraft describes a long arc as it swings around to descend and nail the field perfectly. No jumbojet routine here; instead, a taste of the sweet technology that put a man in the air back in 1903 — only eleven years before the *Empress* last sailed.

Our stopover is brief. "Mont-Joli, 20 minutes, 5000 feet," the co-pilot concisely asserts. Across the St. Lawrence we zoom to our goal, the water a brilliant platinum up westward at the disaster site. The power of life and the power of death come at me now in equal measure; I am keen for this experience.

I am driven to the motel by two of Ballard's assistants, just back from the Black Sea, where he investigated the "Noah's flood" theory of its invasion by salt water. Before that, there was the *Yorktown* shoot (a sunken World War II aircraft carrier located by Ballard) and, off Israel's coast, the oldest deep-water wrecks ever found. This man is everywhere.

"Dr. Ballard always brings people in," says Steve Spencer, his still photographer, concerning my involvement. "On the *Yorktown* shoot we had World War II vets from the US side and the Japanese as well. For emotion."

At the motel, at nearby Ste. Luce-sur-la-Mer, I am introduced to the man himself. Tall, erect, heels together. Assured smile, navy-blue cap. Military presence.

Now it dawns on me: Ballard, perennially front and centre at big newsmaking events, will be so in this shoot as well. Here on Canadian soil, he again quarterbacks a contending team.

He who found the *Titanic* now returns to the world of ocean liners: that will be the documentary's theme. General Douglas MacArthur minus corncob pipe: *I shall return.*

The project is funded by Odyssey Corporation, in which he is co-director along with his wife, Barbara Earle Ballard. The *Empress* will be featured along with two other doomed vessels: the *Titanic* and the torpedo-struck *Lusitania*.

Off to a lobster house we go, with lively talk about those liners of long ago. Ballard bids adieu to them now: "I'm done." To my question about how this feels, he says, "Sombre."

The *Empress* soon comes under scrutiny. When I refer to the cabin number-plate found on the *Storstad's* prow, Ballard mentions the *Stockholm's* penetration by the *Andrea Dorea* — on whose bow, later, was found a child who had been on the liner. Both parents had been with her, and both were killed in the collision.

The human dimension: our talk turns to myth patterns, and Joseph Campbell. "I like the way his mind works," Ballard says, offering me a Campbell quote from Karlfried Graf Durkheim: "When you're on a journey, and the end keeps getting further and further away, then you realize that the real end is the journey."

Mythology is my subject, but I can't recognize the source. *"The Power of Myth!"* says Ballard. Then out come personal details I hadn't known: the death of his son, the breakup of his first marriage. "I needed Campbell at that time."

Storstad after collision.
(George Scott Railton Heritage Centre)

Ballard's lobster arrives, the server advising him to open the white parts first. "I am the surgeon!" says he, embracing this exploratory role. Such high spirits, and spontaneity.

"Guess you're surprised, eh?" says Mark Reynolds, who arranged many details of our shoot. Previously we have discussed media-slants in coverage of the *Empress* story. Some producers will deem it to be "not interesting enough as it is," he says; so they will "constantly seek off-the-cuff remarks."

Mark requires any questions about his dives to be submitted in advance. I opt now for greater freedom of access: whatever is asked about the *Empress*, I'll simply speak from the heart. A bit risky, but so what.

With Peter Schnall I raise the issue of media bias. He says, forthcomingly, that you can do virtually anything to distort the truth.

We talk about Sergei Eisenstein's montage theory — how the same footage placed in different contexts will take different meanings. Film of a laughing man will suggest benevolence when shown after a scene of innocent childen; the same footage shown after a scene of cruelty will make him appear sadistic. It all depends on the context, over which I have no control.

Having discussed tricks of the game, I find it easier to relax with Peter. Everything seems up-front, although I well expect to be the prey in a cat-and-mouse game later on.

Mark introduces me to the legendary Philippe Beaudry: six hundred dives of the *Empress*, collecting *Empress* items for twenty-nine years. He who goes to the limit and then some, *au bout*, is an engaging man with a quirky sense of humour.

Beaudry's *Empress* enthusiasm led to the Musée de la Mer's foundation. At its opening a speech was given by William Tantum IV who, at 7, was with his father on a St. Lawrence cruise aboard the steamer *Duchess of Athol* when she rammed and sank the collier *Maine*. Conversation turned to the *Empress*, stirring Tantum so deeply that he later had an early book on the disaster republished. Tantum also dreamed of finding the *Titanic* — and predicted that Ballard would be the one to succeed.

Ballard recalls Tantum's passion for shipwrecks: "I was a geologist, and ocean liners didn't mean very much until I met him." The military had been paramount for Tantum until a debilitating wound deflected his interests toward those old liners; he gave many acquaintances a sense that they should be preserved.

I mention reference to Tantum in Ballard's *The Discovery of the Titanic*: "Gradually, largely through his influence, the ship became much more than something to find in deep water. As he recreated the *Titanic*'s final hours, she began to take on a personality — to develop a soul." Did this man, in whose memory Ballard left a plaque on the *Titanic*, serve as a second father?

"Perhaps," he allows.

Then, time for my big *faux pas*: mentioning a well-known *Titanic* book written by someone identifying himself as Dr. Charles Pellegrino.

Well, this man was *not* a doctor, Ballard explains, and did *not* write anything but lies. "Do you remember *Charlie?*" he calls down the table to someone, underlining what I take to be the uncanonicity of mentioning Pellegrino's name.

Now wait a minute. I am here to assist in an area painful to myself, and can hardly be expected to know all the protocol and taboos. So I boldly go on to ask about details in Pellegrino's book, and we pursue several of them: fascinating talk.

We ponder questions about the *Empress*. The *Storstad*'s prow coming loose from the cavity in her side. The red and green lights of both vessels. The real cause of disaster. Going over the events, I conclude as usual that the truth will remain a mystery, now and forever.

Ballard ponders how these ships, essentially for immigrants, might be filled on the return trip to England. Having perused the *Empress's* passenger list, I suggest that Third Class was fully booked with those desiring passage back to the old land for a renewal of ties.

Hannah circulates *Till We Meet Again* by Herbert Wood, a close friend of many who sailed on the *Empress*. His book now gets low grades, for lack of technical data. Yet I cherish this account by someone so intimately linked with the events. It is Wood who retells Major Simco's premonition of the corpses, adding that a few Salvationists cancelled their sailing when they heard it:

> *In the water itself, people were struggling. Some broke through the procession. Their faces were horrible, frantic with fear and pain, distorted with frenzy. Some had torn flesh; others, twisted limbs. It was ghastly!*

The next day, Ballard often sings the start of our national anthem: "Oh . . . Caaaah . . . Na-dah." He tells a joke about the name's origin: a Newfie, undone by our well-known verbal tic, says, "C — eh? N — eh? D — eh?"

Here is an unexpected side of the man I had known merely as an explorer; "explorer," in fact, is the word Ballard wishes to have inscribed on his tombstone. A secretary of the navy, John Lehman, once praised him as a lower-depths counterpart to Tom Cruise in *Top Gun*, and presented him with a baseball cap with the title "Bottom Gun."

The day being too windy for the first dives, Peter shoots footage of *Empress* burial sites. Lunch is taken here aboard our imposing yacht, the *Night Wind*, then we return to the motel for footage of the family photos I have brought along.

Peter spreads the album on a table, and gently leafs through its pages. A portrait of the young Bertha is placed below the lens. My ancestor, now to be known by a wider public.

David often sailed on the big liners, she had never done so. "I'll take your mother to England, show her the Army," he is said to have told the children. It was settled: both David and Bertha would attend the Congress.

"Really secure motel room, camera doesn't jump around," says Peter. Hmmmmmmmmmmmmmmmm-click. Two down. Then the Sussex group portrait, David and the closest of kin. I give Hannah the names.

And now that 1914 Last Photo — the one displayed on living-room pianos, by which the next generation would learn about a ship called the *Empress of Ireland*. Bertha and David sit among their offspring, arranged in order of age. There is a glow, an energy, in these people, four of whom wear the Army uniform.

Family of David and Bertha Creighton, 1914.

At upper left is Wilfred, a Staff Band member, who agreed to stay behind "just in case." Edith, especially luminous in this portrait, stands alongside my father. Bertha holds Arthur, aged 8. Four-year-old Cyrus, in a flowing bandana, sits with the father he has only begun to know.

"Thank you, David. Beautiful photos," says Peter at the end. I express my appreciation for his interest in them.

Amid late-afternoon radiance we do a take at Ste. Luce Church, which holds no connection to the *Empress* but is picturesque. The light is best right now, says Ballard. "Symbolism."

Here I am to be filmed reading David's last letter, completed on the boat and mailed at Rimouski. It is addressed to Wilfred and signed by both parents, though clearly penned by the father. I take it out for a read-through:

Canadian Pacific Railway
Atlantic Service

R M S Empress of Ireland
May 28, 1914
My Dear Son:

We were so pleased to get your wire and to learn that all were well. May the dear Lord, whom I humbly endeavour to serve and whom you also strive to follow, abundantly bless you & Edith & Willie & Arthur & Cyrus & give us in due time the pleasure of meeting again with good news & all well.

I do believe you will all honestly strive to be helpful to each other & do your best during our absence. It was really brave of you all.

I had a frightfully busy trip down and right up to this minute. We are now sailing down along the St Lawrence & I hope to mail this from Rimouski everything is going very nicely and the day has been beautiful . . . We will have a good budget of news to mail you when we land at Liverpool.

Our very best affection & love for all. Let the others read this letter.

Papa & Mama

On the rocky shoreline, where somebody's jacket has been placed on a hummock, I sit for the take. Exposure meter out, mike boom lowered.

Jerry now takes over the camera, Peter, crouching alongside, asks, "How do you feel at this moment?" Sentiment, something to come through on the TV screen. The most basic of messages, to reach that hypothetically average viewer at which the market is aimed.

Here also in my hand is a two-page account that I wrote to encompass the disaster's main aspects. My feelings are wrapped up in this. I plunge in, with things that happened and were said.

Partisan Pictures shoot in Ste. Luce-sur-la-Mer, August 1999.
(Steve Spencer)

"Never mind that piece of paper," says Peter. Okay; I put it down and words come from my mouth — none of which, not one, can I later recall.

At the motel as we are about to go for dinner, Peter tries for sunset footage at our beach. Waiting, waiting. Rays spread from the clouds in an upside-down V: shoot. Light strengthens to create golden bars along the water: shoot.

Five crew members come down to be with him. Finally the tripod is folded. And just now the sun gains a vast sovereignty of gold: stunning. Should have waited.

But Peter only smiles, the ruddy glow reflecting on his face. "There's a sunset every day," he says — and then, "Quite a river you have here."

Restaurant selection is by Jay Minkin, our exuberant video technician, who leads us to a Cambodian place, *Le Lotus*. Here the server, struggling with our tongue, is congratulated for "speaking English well" — in French Canada, the ultimate gaffe.

Roulleaux being on the menu, Ballard recalls a Rolex commercial he once ill-advisedly agreed to. He wore a Rolex on something wrongly identified, in the proofs, as a "submersible." Out went a correction, several times — *IT-IS-NOT-A-SUBMERSIBLE* — but the ad was run as such, just the same. Who cares about the truth?

"I get a letter every day from someone wanting me to raise some plane or other," he laughs. He is also plagued by maniacs. One neo-Nazi, upset that Ballard discovered the *Bismarck* and thus defiled a sacred site, came at him in a motorcycle. Not much fun to be famous.

Conversation lacks the first night's vitality, and I miss that. There is a hierarchy of important things, with Canada well down the scale. Of course, these are hard-working people who need relaxation more than a lot of heavy talk.

I mention the proximity of Partisan's offices to Herman Melville's final abode, over on 26th Street. Hoping to talk about Captain Ahab and his crew, I refer to their whaler, the *Pequod* — only to have someone insist that it was called the *Essex*. This puts me briefly on the spot; then we get away from Melville's world entirely.

I wish we could fully enter into some topic, any topic pertaining to our film. The deeper meaning of those liners, of ocean ventures, of human will, of accident and folly. But everyone seems a little down, with no filming of *Empress* dives yet and two of the five days gone.

SOMEBODY'S BAD LUCK

The last lurch came, and they were flung into the seething waters. Their bodies were washed ashore, encased in caskets of crystal ice, which speedily dissolved, but their names are covered with honour that is imperishable.
British *War Cry*, June 6, 1914

ERFECT MORNING FOR A shoot: sunshine, hardly any wind, the water brilliant. We head out in our big expensive boat. Yvon Vannin, who totally rebuilt the *Night Wind*, captains it now. Handsome and keen, a Rocket Richard of the boat trade.

"It's a diving day today," says Réal Gagnon, his helmsman. Quebeckers at the wheel; two of the divers Anglo- Canadian; Americans running the show. This is like a World War II movie, with ethnic types and lots of verve.

The *Night Wind* slows to a stop, is anchored. Quietness. Yvon, out on deck now, shows me our alignment with the shore: "You see it like that, you're right on top of the wreck." The *wreck*: this doesn't quite register.

Jay, handling video transmissions from below, comes into his

Yvon Vannin and Real Gagnon. (David Creighton)

own. He is beside himself with joy. "What a day!" he cries. "Break out the champagne!"

At this moment I break down, sobbing like a baby — only a minute or so, the usual length at such times. And not with any resentment that he forgot the dead. Because I felt the same way.

After a decent interval Peter is before me with the camera. "Something happened just then, David," says he. "How do you feel now?" I fulfill what seems necessary to bring the *Empress* onto television screens.

The power of life and the power of death, again in equal measure.

I become absorbed in the roles played by these people working on our film. They all seem so innocent, so admirable. Bob Cranston, preparing to operate the underwater camera, tells me that all this started for him in San Diego with his first dives, at 9 or 10: "It's what I've always been doing."

Glen, picking up sound with his mike-on-a-fishing-pole, defines our media concern: "the most significant thing at the moment." Taking an emotive soundbite from me would be like hooking a good-sized trout. Life, reality.

Réal, on the bridge, explains how the depth-indicator picks up the *Empress*: "You see eighty-four feet — that's the top of the boat. Might be eighty-five, depending on the tides."

Ballard oversees all. A cellphone message comes for him: *USA Today*, running a Life section piece. "Do you remember them interviewing you?" Barbara asks.

Robert Ballard and
Barbara Earle Ballard.
(David Creighton)

"Hello, you fishes — fishy fish?" says Jay to the realms below. A sound like bones rattling together begins: "Somebody's cold down there — you hear that?" His lingo gives no problem now, I've adjusted. I rather like his sense of drama and strangeness.

All these levels at which I experience the boat: visual, mental, emotional.

"I'll be down there with my gear," Bob explains to another diver. "I'll jump in the water and you hand me the camera and we'll turn the light on."

"Sound just rolled out," Glen reports. The divers, poised for the plunge, wait longer as the new tape is fitted in.

"And I need a new mag," Peter laughs. Finally, everything's set. *Splash! Splash!*

We go inside to watch the monitor. "You can sit here if you like, David," Peter suggests, motioning to a stool in front. Time for a few reaction shots.

On the screen I see tiny divers' lamps down in the labyrinth, the place of darkness. Ethereal, these backlit particles resembling cumulus clouds.

But there is not enough power. Ballard speaks into a thin mike: "We've done everything we can do re lights. . . . Are they on now? . . . Bob . . . are . . . your . . . lights . . . still . . . off? Over . . . . Roger that, we understand that . . . Roger roger we are troubleshooting that."

World War II again, Ballard manning PT-109 as tension mounts. "Bob, we're at the end of your tether — over . . . . Is he on the wreck? . . . . What is the problem, the power or the connections? . . . We see your image."

Bottom Gun: be sure he will find the glitch. Yes: lights on. "Cool!" Jay shouts.

"They did the test on the dock, on the *dock!*" Ballard exclaims in disgust. We have power, but also a loose connection within the boat: "Everybody's got to be careful going down those steps!"

He and I stare at the monitor as Bob explores the *Empress's* bow, Peter and Steve shooting away at us. Media reverberation: photos taken of people being filmed while watching video.

"We need to iris up your light because there's not much light," says Ballard. "Now we're talking. . . . Wow, look at that growth! . . . Shallow-level dive, the difference between the *Yorktown* and this. . . ."

A big furry sea monster. Down where my grandparents were promoted to glory.

Ballard asks for a copy of his book *Lost Liners* to consult Ken Marschall's sunken-*Empress* painting, the one owned by Mark. He manages to find shapes like those on the picture: "Bob's following a handrail — if I was on the *Titanic* I'd know . . . ."

The two of us, I gather, are to comment knowledgeably on what is seen now. Up in the broadcast booth at Superbowl time, smooth on the uptake — except that my mind is on other things.

"Looks like he's on the riveted hull," Ballard suggests. Wait a minute — I'm trying to remember something Mark told me. Wait a minute, I've actually got something to say.

"The *Empress* and *Titanic* are much the same," I remark in all casualness, "same general structure, same fixtures." Thank God something is on tape now to lift me above duncecap level.

"I suspect they've used up their bottom time," says Ballard.

"See how green that water is — like the *Lusitania.*" *You're right, Bob, just like the* Lusitania — *over.*

Now I withdraw. Impossible to sit with the others for lunch, chatting about this and that. I retreat to the bow, the farthest point away from film production. If someone comes along, fine, but I'm not budging.

Réal appears after a while, humorously needling me about the food I've missed. *Just not very hungry right now, thanks.*

We talk about traffic lines on the river. They're further out than before, further out than when the *Empress of Ireland* sank.

She went down in fourteen minutes, says Réal, knowing that I need to talk about it. "People down below, right here," he says; all the panic and terror. "Over there at Pointe-au-Père, that's where the pilot's boat went, just before."

The pilot's cutter, *Eureka*, returned as usual on that long ago May 29. At Pointe-au-Père's Marconi shore station, all was normal until 1:56 a.m., when an anxious message came from the *Empress.*

Five minutes later an SOS arrived: she was going down.

Réal places a hand on my shoulder: "Anyway, enjoy the sunshine — while we're still alive!" One of the most eloquent sentences I've ever heard.

Canadian Pacific's long-time telegraph operator at Pointe-au-Père, John McWilliams, could scarcely believe it. On this calm night, such sudden disaster? He tapped out a reply, and despatched the mail steamer *Lady Evelyn*, just returned to Rimouski Wharf.

At 2:30 the *Eureka* was also sent out. Its captain, Jean Baptiste Belanger, had helped to seize Hawley Crippen only four years before — the arrest that gave worldwide fame to Captain Kendall of the *Empress*.

The *Eureka*'s crew received the first direct view of catastrophe — a lifeboat, in which someone cried out, "For God's sake hurry up, there are thousands drowning just ahead." But nearly all in the river were already dead.

A diver is still below, right at the prow. Bubbles denote the breathing.

Beautifully they wobble up, one or two or three or four or five or six at a time, to fountain on the surface. There is a living presence down there.

How few realized the danger, how swiftly they were engulfed, how final their doom.

My grandfather often sailed these ships on his round of duties, knew them intimately. In an emergency he would have understood the need to get right up onto the deck. But we have no clear evidence of any such effort by David and Bertha on that night. They never had the power to move.

"Most of them were in their cabins and could not get out because of the terrible rush of water," said Major George Attwell, who managed to struggle onto the deck with Mary. "As the great, dripping black hull rolled, we came nearer and nearer to its keel. Then it sank."

Band Sergeant John Fowler, a light sleeper, had actually glimpsed the *Storstad* through his porthole. "I saw a big black shape loom up suddenly," he said. Then the jolt: "It was more of a grinding sensation, and before I realized what had happened, my cabin began to fill with water."

Captain Rufus Spooner, managing to get onto the hull, saw "a terrific explosion of air and steam" from a porthole. A huge wave made by the keel swept him toward someone on top of a table;

"Don't come near me or you'll drown me!" this man kept saying, before being struck by an object that threw him down. Spooner made it to an upturned lifeboat, clinging there until rescued.

Major Turpin also reached a lifeboat, just as someone cried, "Oh, look, there she goes." He turned to watch, "and a long low moan, more like a sigh, broke from her crowded, upturned side." Silence abruptly fell, then there were the wails of the drowning: "If I could forget that awful cry!"

Yvon comes along. All I need now is ordinary human contact, and this is what he provides. Yvon owns the marina, and there is a lot about that we can discuss. And about the *Night Wind*, all the things he did to reconstruct it. All the materials — teak, for instance.

Somebody approached Yvon once with a load of teak, and he asked where it came from. It was from the *Empress of Ireland*. "Get out of here with that teak and never show your face again," he said. "You take somebody's bad luck and make money from it."

Then Yvon says that he will never see the movie *Titanic*, as it amounts to the same thing. I don't have the will to pose the obvious question: Why we are all here now, but to gain also from somebody's bad luck? It is easy to rationalize this, but the question remains.

"Some people think they're better than God — no fear," he goes on, referring to shipwrecks that continue to happen hereabouts. A friend, a scallop fisherman, went out last year on December 5. "Pierre, you'll kill yourself!" said Yvon, and he was right: this man's boat was crushed by the ice.

Survival: Canada as Margaret Atwood sees it. John Franklin and all his crew. Never have I felt so Canadian as at this moment, talking with a Quebecker about this. "We're not so good as we think," says Yvon.

I am in the film because my *grandmère* and *grandpère* are down there now, I tell him; they will interview me and ask *what do I feel* and when I display emotion, they are finished. Yvon grins and dips a finger in his mouth to mime the required tears.

Nothing filmically expressed by Canadians about the ship has gone beyond the humdrum. And now, an American crew pours its own syrup over this particular stack of pancakes.

Until last year, at 53, Yvon was an ardent skier. Always he felt the adrenalin high — "too difficult . . . no, it will be exciting . . . I fear this

. . . no, just push off" — and once in soft snow he could not keep his feet together, so as to mangle a knee which now must be rebuilt. A second of incertitude brought ruin — for Yvon as for the *Empress*.

He leaves me now, as the afternoon calm deepens. An uncanny shimmer is upon everything.

Staff Bandsman Ernest Green looked like the young Laurence Olivier. He was a friend of artist Teddy Gray, whose editorial cartoons appeared in *The Toronto Star;* often he sketched Green as an archetype of the Salvation Army warrior.

Family of
Adjutant Harry Green.
(George Scott Railton
Heritage Centre)

Ernest loved his sister Jenny and his parents, Adjutant and Mrs. Green. They were lost, but handsome Ernie Green was among the few who survived. He did so by grasping the lifebelt of a man already dead.

"Well, whatever happens, my boy," his father had said as the boat sank, "we are in God's hands." Green vowed to consecrate his life, if spared, to God's service as a Salvation Army officer. And so he did.

Green later gave this image of disaster: "a village suddenly flooded and all the people floating in the water." He remembered the faces of those seen "bobbing up and down with the ship gone underneath and only water."

Ballard comes by, the afternoon still nearly windless. "A sea of glass," says he in mock-documentary tones. "We do not attack the sea, we make loooooove to the sea."

Peter also lingers for a while, again wondering how I feel. "I feel cold, I've been shivering for hours even in the heat." Why? "In sympathy, I think."

A whale is spotted toward land. More inquiry now from Peter — a question is asked, it sinks in, the camera runs, I find what to say, out it comes, the take runs on, finally they have enough.

Ballard is now with me at the prow and I ask what he means in *The Discovery of the Titanic* — sailing away from that wreck "as if those who perished aboard the *Titanic* could finally rest." It was a granting of peace, he explains. For me here, I reply, it is simply a matter of coming to terms with what happened.

Ballard offers two flower bouquets for me to toss onto the waters. He comments on how beautiful the flowers look as they descend. I am expected to say something apt. Like going to the mercy seat, and giving testimony before all.

The diving now finished, we head back to port along paths taken by the *Lady Evelyn* and *Eureka*, bearing the survivors.

Those reaching the *Storstad* were given clothing by the crew. Virtually everything but what they wore went to the survivors, until none was left. Green was naked except for a towel around his midriff: "I was penniless, homeless and clothless."

There were many tales to be told. "She gave a hiss and a gurgle before sinking," bandsman Bert Greenaway recounted. "I saw scores swimming about, calling for help. Some of them when rescued went crazy."

Lieutenant Alf Keith spoke of an explosion that erupted when water struck the boilers: "The ship seemed to rear a little; then all went down." Yet he made it to the *Storstad*, attiring himself in the tablecloth now displayed at the Railton Centre.

Grace Hanagan had lost consciousness, and woke up in a bed on the *Storstad*, asking for her mother. An officer promised to find her, and Grace clung to that promise even after being shown her father's body in a Toronto mortuary. For years she suffered nightmares and "a great fear and terror of a tap running." Hearing a bathtub being filled, the grown woman would again experience the panic of going down in the water.

Homeward bound. Ballard, at the prow, is filmed from the Zodiac inflatable racing alongside. "Do a 90-degree turn and go straight for the sun," he commands. Well done. "Now we all look pretty!" he amiably adds.

My last morning here, more humid than before, gives that northwoods aroma remembered from the *dîner-bénéfice* night. As I walk down to the water, a salt aroma supplants it; returning, I experience the reverse. I amuse myself by going from one to the other. Sweet, salt; salt, sweet; sweet, salt.

At our breakfast spot Ballard talks about Charles Lindbergh, whose new biography he has read. Steven Biel suggests that Ballard himself was a kind of Lindbergh, greeted by thousands at Woods Hole after finding the greatest of lost liners; thus he "brought the *Titanic*'s maiden voyage to a long-awaited end."

I see Ballard more in terms of Tom Sawyer, who gained funding through wily persuasion: it's *good* to labour at painting a fence and then to stand back and admire the result. Just as it would be *good* to finance the discovery of the *Titanic, good* for PBS to fund our *Empress* dive. No pain at all.

Time to say goodbye. In my copy of *The Discovery of the Titanic*, Ballard writes, "I enjoyed our journey together." We gather for a group photo before a taxi picks up Steve and me for the Montreal flight.

Back home, I describe Ballard to my wife Judy, an admirer of rugged-American-hero types — Clint Eastwood, Bruce Springsteen, George Clooney, Sam Shepard — and she duly ranks him among these: "Coolness during emergency, scientific background, technical proficiency — *The Right Stuff*, all that plus high-spiritedness."

I phone my brother Fred to tell about the shoot, and he interjects the low bursts of laughter reserved for something far-out.

Partisan Pictures shoot, Rimouski, August 1999.
(Steve Spencer)

Nothing seems to have slighted our family or the Salvation Army, I tell him. But I'm not entirely sure.

My cousin Robert, Arthur's son, knows about documentaries, having been in several dealing with cranial-facial surgery at the Hospital for Sick Children, where he is anesthetist-in-chief. "They must be hugging themselves to have found someone really interested in the subject," he says — a welcome kind of reassurance.

Tonight I have a dream:

I am in my study, Judy upstairs in the kitchen (or approximations thereof). Anxiously she tells me that x is here to see me. I am not concerned, but glad to have x come by. I hold out my hand as he comes down to my study. He ignores it, brushing on past into our bedroom.

I see that x is not the man I thought he was, but one bearing a sharp grievance. Arriving with him is a Hogarthian set of people in devotional attitudes. They are followers of x. All seem menacing but somewhat crazy, one especially so in a cloying, jellylike way.

I grasp that my transgression, being so blatant, calls for huge recompense. But x never does reappear to exact it. I suffer only the tumult of deranged people invading our space.

144

REMEMBER THEM IN THE ETERNAL CITY

DURING TORONTO'S GREAT MEMORIAL Service, the deepest emotion came when the wife of Major George Attwell, Mary, rose to speak even though "evidently suffering greatly from nervous shock." She spoke of happiness that spread through the party as their liner sailed along the St. Lawrence.

"The moon was shining down, and everything was peaceful and lovely. The boat was silently gliding through the water." With sobs often rising to her throat, she spoke of friends sitting in a shady nook of the boat. Their names came to her lips: Mrs. Rees, Mrs. Maidment, Mrs. Simco — and also Bertha Creighton, in the only known eyewitness account of her final hours.

"A beautiful breeze blew gently, and the band played a number of songs," said Mrs. Attwell. "The band finished and the last I heard them play was 'Sweet and Low.' We sat for a time, loth to leave, until presently the Commissioner came along and said to his wife, 'My dear, you must come away, you'll be tired tomorrow.' It's splendid to remember them like that — and I shan't forget Mrs. Rees's quiet smile at our happiness."

She turned away from the audience to rest her shaken voice, and went on. "I would like to talk to you about the end. It was like awaiting — awaiting. A few spoke to me before that last plunge until the ship went down — no cries — just a sob, just a sigh."

Then Mrs. Attwell gave the mourners an image of departure. "It's not death — it is just as if a large door had been opened and they had passed out," she told them. "Do not remember them in the water: remember them in the Eternal City."

PART FOUR

The Black Dinner

CRYSTAL PALACE DAY

*Rousing marches and impetuous dithyrambs rise to the heavens
from people among whom the depressing noise called "sacred
music" is a standing joke; a flag with Blood and Fire on it is
unfurled, not in murderous rancour, but because fire is beautiful
and blood a vital and splendid red . . . .*

George Bernard Shaw,
Preface to *Major Barbara*

I N SEPTEMBER, HUNGER FOR more *Empress* background draws me to
London on a Canadian Airlines jet. Without incident I span the
Atlantic, eighty-five years after my grandparents' failed voyage.

By tube I reach the suburb of Sydenham, where the 1914
Congress had its peak moment — Crystal Palace Day. The site of
this iron-and-glass marvel, destroyed by fire in 1936, is revealed by
stone arcades from which it arose. A colossal head of the Palace's
gifted architect, Joseph Paxton, has been erected by the former
entrance. My 1911 *Baedeker's London and its Environs* sets the scene:

> *The principal attractions are the palace itself, as an interesting
> example of glass and iron construction, its imposing and
> tastefully arranged interior, the excellent casts of notable works
> of architecture and scupture, the beautiful gardens, and, in
> summer 1911, the Festival of Empire.*

Festival of Empire: coincidentally, right now in London hooplah is
given to a colossal Millenium Dome meant to celebrate British
achievement. That earlier gala was also of large dimensions, as my
Baedeker shows: "In the gardens numerous imposing pavilions have been
erected, linked by 1 1/2 M of electric railway, passing through scenic
reproductions of life in various parts of the British Empire. There is to
be also a Pageant of London and the Empire, with 15,000 performers."

For fifty thousand Salvationists gathered here in 1914, "Crystal
Palace Day" was itself a Festival of Empire. It began with an impressive
flag-hoisting rite. "When the flags which separate people were all

bravely flying, the one which unites all nations of the earth was run up," said the *War Cry*, referring to the Army's red-yellow-blue banner.

Delegates on the platform later gave vent to utterances typical of their nation: "the mountain calls of the Swiss, the 'coo-ee' of the Australian bush, the 'Herai-mai' of the Maori." Once, to the crowd's delight, Booth linked arms with a Zulu and a Javanese.

Congress delegates would have acquired much the same romantic vision of Empire as I did, in Toronto's school system a quarter-century later. With the bad parts airbrushed out: as when imperial troops slaughtered 10,000 Zulus "for no other offence," said statesman William Gladstone, "than their attempt to defend against your artillery with their naked bodies, their hearths and their homes, their wives and families."

The Palace site crowns a hill, and descending its slope I come to a smaller glass-and-metal structure, the Crystal Palace National Sports Centre. A computer fair occurs here today.

In 1914 the weather cleared for a grand music festival held in numerous venues on the grounds hereabouts, over 150 bands "rousing the neighbourhood with joyful trumpetings."

A football field was the scene of a two-mile afternoon March Past featuring Newfoundland sealers, "much befeathered Redskins from Canada," Scots in tartan sashes, rickshaw boys, South African natives representing witch doctors.

All this pomp of imperialism, before it was no longer a glory but a crime.

The delegation from India boasted the colouful Kala, "an industrious member of The Army's Settlement for ex-criminals in the Punjab," whose first act on arriving at the settlement had been "to catch, kill, and eat the Officer's cat." On this occasion he "danced about like a child attending its first school treat." General Bramwell Booth himself gladdened the crowd when he "took a baby from the arms of its mother and danced it in an ecstasy of joy."

Zulus "gave voice to a fearful war whoop, jumped several feet in the air, brandished their weapons, rushed round the stand and then passed on with the march." American cowboys rode wildly into the field, "shouting in such an exhilarating manner that the crowd took up the refrain."

Germany's Salvationists formed "the most martial section," said the *War Cry*. "Clad in uniforms of vivid blue and red, it marched with splendid eclat and mien." Yet the day's participants were seen as "engaged in solving the problem of racial differences and in heralding the dawn of a new era — the universal brotherhood of man."

The Palace's 300,000 window panes formed the world's largest enclosed space, and when the Salvationists held an evening service here its higher parts initially stood out "transparent against the afterglow of the vanished sun." The General, stirred by the great crowd, took up a large megaphone to give his message of faith. "I want you to help us — so that the whole world shall see our colours waving. Good night, God bless you for ever and ever!"

"And you!" echoed back the crowd in a roar that merged with victorious song as the band played, "Praise God from Whom all Blessings Flow."

Paxton's wondrous creation as it stood in 1851, housing the Great Exhibition with 100,000 displays proclaiming material progress, is described in Fyodor Dostoevsky's *Notes from Underground*. For his "Underground Man," the Crystal Palace projects false dreams of a rational utopia. "Reason," he says, "only satisfies the rational side of human nature, while desire manifests life itself."

The Palace's "mathematical exactitude" implies freedom from suffering; "and yet I'm sure man will never renounce real suffering — that is, destruction and chaos." The Underground Man visualizes all earthly blessings floating down some day — "and even then, out of sheer ingratitude and spite, man will play a nasty trick on you." Cleopatra enjoyed sticking pins in her slaves' breasts, he recalls — golden pins idly jabbed into people to relieve the boredom.

Dostoevsky was a Christian who believed in the Fall, who regarded suffering as the inevitable product of irrational whim, who saw the point of existence as salvation through love. Those Salvationists of 1914 might have agreed. *Don't cut off your nose to spite your face*, said my grandmother, who failed to experience Crystal Palace Day because of a whim felt by nature on that St. Lawrence shipping lane.

Four-letter graffiti of recent creation — PEST, TEAK, FUME, FINE, MERK, ZIMA, DARK, MEMO — abound on the train line back from Crystal Palace Park. I take the tube to the Palace's original site, in Hyde Park.

On opening day Victoria made her way to a throne beneath a giant elm, amazingly preserved under the glass, amid displays of thirteen thousand exhibitors confirming England's manufacturing prowess. The world's first industrial nation controlled one-third of all international trade. And it undertook to "civilize" the globe.

Today the long oval site is swept by a tractor-drawn mower, sending up a trail of dust. Its operator well knows about the Palace — built, he explains, on rubble that has now subsided. "It's all settled so much now that junk is starting to poke through."

Nearby stands the Albert Memorial, commissioned by Victoria as a shrine to the Prince Consort's memory — warmly regarded now, after decades of ridicule as the epitome of Victorian-Gothic kitsch. Grief-stricken at her husband's death, she closed off the world until Prime Minister Benjamin Disraeli bestowed an august title: "Empress of India."

At Albert Hall, opposite, soon to unfold is the Last Night at the Proms, with "Rule Britannia" lustily sung as in imperial times. Last Nights are staged all over the world now, I remark to a woman buying her ticket. "And all over England!" she adds, with a grimace.

The Congress's *Empress* memorial day, held at Albert Hall, was recounted in the *War Cry*. "A distant piping breaks in upon the unfathomable silence": the Canadian contingent — those arriving on boats other than the *Empress* — entered the hall and General Booth, in a voice "tremulous with suppressed feelings," placed death in its true context:

> *We feel that they have entered into that great world of reality, they have passed from the shadow to the substance. Their temptations are all behind, their tears are wiped away, their Saviour is in the midst.*

A half-century earlier William Booth had come from the Midlands to London's most crime-ridden slum, Mile End, intent on reaching the larger masses. Here, half expecting to find scenes of degradation, I am brought up to date by a local man. "Booth — when he was about, it was *bad*: pickpockets, murderers!" says he, chopping the air with his hand. "But it all changed after the war. Now, you might pay 200,000 pounds for a place that's been fixed up."

I walk down Mile End Road to a battleship-grey statue of the Founder bearing a simple text: "Here William Booth commenced the work of the Salvation Army July 1865." He is shown with an index finger extended — today, toward the Empire Fish and Chips / Chinese takeout — and with a long flowing beard.

Booth admired the early Christians' faith for its simplicity — and the British Empire for its vast military structures. What wonders might be achieved by Salvationist warriors obedient to their captains? Ministering to "the wounded and dying on the battlefields of life," he slept for months with a British Army manual at bedside.

Booth, marshalling former prostitutes and wife-beaters and thieves into a force for good, was perpetually under attack by the law and the lawless alike. Once, when Evangeline Booth was felled by a stone, a constable tried to place against *her* a disorderly conduct charge — which his superior officer gallantly refused to support.

At a Quaker burial ground, meetings were held in a circus tent soon blown down by the wind, whereupon the faithful "fell back on our cathedral, the open air." Copthorn Homes has a sign on the site today, promising that three-bedroom townhouses will soon be available here. "Trendy area, close to the City," says a passerby, jerking his thumb westward.

William Booth was the Army's shaman, leading it into spirit worlds. Consider a 1902 Message given in Toronto as recalled by his travelling companion, F. Hayter Fox: "Whither is he taking us? Towards the flickering gleam of Hell we descend, plunging down, ever down . . . Massey Hall fades from view." In imagination Booth discerns Judas Iscariot, counting his pieces of silver: "AH!!! THAT WAS WHAT I SOLD HEAVEN FOR — THAT WAS WHAT I SOLD MY SOUL FOR." Paradise forfeited, through greed. "What shall a man give in exchange for his soul?" asks the General. "What are you giving? You, you, YOU?"

At the Army's heritage centre near St. Paul's I chat with a curator, Miriam, about Booth's 1891 best-seller, *In Darkest England, and the Way Out*. It marked an historic moment, when Booth began to favour social work as spelled out in its pages.

"So, you would like to see the book?" asks Miriam. *In Darkest England*, that Blake-like vision of masses transformed by greed, is soon on my desk. I unfold a multi-hued frontispiece showing waves marked "drunkenness," "despair," "harlots," "wife desertion," "starvation," "rape," "prison," "brothels," "slavery," "illegitimacy," "betting." A small-print Key to the Chart explains this scene:

> In the raging Sea, surrounding the Salvation Lighthouse, are to
> be seen the victims of vice and poverty who are sinking to ruin,
> but whom the Officers appointed to carry out the Scheme are
> struggling to save.

Receiving a laser photocopy of the frontispiece, a minor masterpiece of design, I notice that it is unsigned. "They were very modest in those days," says Miriam. "Nothing belonged to a person — all belonged to the big thing, were dedicated to it."

In Darkest England proposed deliverance: "Drawing up these poor outcasts, reforming them, and creating in them habits of industry, honesty and truth." The machine devoured human lives, otherwise nurtured in wholesome rural communities. People must be returned to farmland and radiant sunshine, said Booth, anticipating Joni Mitchell's imagery: "Back again to the Garden!"

In Darkest England opened a heroic new mission for the Army's personnel. Yet this was viewed as a "change of mind" from Booth's initial soul-saving mission by Army trailblazer George Railton. In 1894 he learned that Army life-insurance policies would be sold — Salvationists, for whom death meant everlasting glory, saving against future uncertainties! — and decided to stage a protest.

He entered a major Army meeting barefoot and in sackcloth. Just like Railton to act so eccentrically, some laughed. Then he rose, at testimony time, to speak. "I was so glad to hear our General in the holiness meeting this morning lay down the principles of self-sacrifice which he deemed necessary for successful salvation warfare," said he. "Judge then my surprise when I found lying at my feet a dirty piece of paper."

Brandishing an advertisement for the insurance plan, Railton spoke of the "thirty-three farthings yearly in return" that beneficiaries would receive, then trampled the handbill underfoot. Many took his side, but the official opinion was that overwork had brought on "mental strain."

Now social work — rescue homes, food and shelter depots, workshops, salvage brigades — came to the fore. In Darkest England's frontispiece shows a "colony across the sea," much resembling Canada, with steamers crossing to this land of "farm colonies."

Frontispiece to William Booth's *In Darkest England, and the Way Out*
(1891).

These would be founded by immigration officers "whose business it will be to acquire every kind of information as to suitable countries and the openings they present for different trades and callings." Here is what drew my grandfather to his ultimate task.

And in London, arranging transportation, he must have often visited 62 Charing Cross Road, now a used-book shop. Here, as my 1911 *Baedeker* states, is where Canadian Pacific then had a ticket office:

> *Canadian Pacific Railway ("C. P. R.") Steamers belonging to this company ply from Montreal every Thurs. in summer, from Saint John every Sat. in winter, for Liverpool, returning every Frid. or Tuesday. Saloon-fare from 45, second cabin from 37 dollars. Offices, 62 Charing Cross, S. W., and 67 King William St., E. C., "Empress of Britain", "Empress of Ireland" (each 14,600 tons) "Lake Manitoba".*

The Salvation Army's imperial vision reflected that of Britain as a whole. Then came the war, which changed everything. The term *empress*, along with *empire* and *imperialist*, gained negative connotations.

So the liner *Empress of Ireland* would now be recalled, if at all, as something from an old order best forgotten.

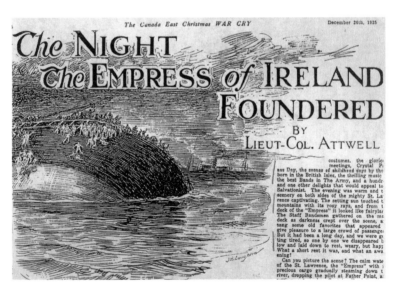

Heading for *War Cry* article by George Attwell, 1925.

And those retelling the tragedy would mute the terror. Major Attwell, having at first told about that horrifying inrush of water, gave another remembrance in 1925. He spoke of the voyagers' happiness at their first glimpse of their *Empress* cabins, "and the sense of satisfaction at the thought that there seemed to be nothing to mar our comfort."

Attwell saw himself among the Congress delegates once more in the Second Class dining room, making "a brilliant picture in our uniforms." The British Empire was still secure, and all spoke jubilantly about what seemed to lie ahead:

> *the delegations from every country in the world, the strange costumes, the glorious meetings, Crystal Palace Day, the scenes of childhood days by those born in the British Isles, the thrilling music by the best bands in The Army, and a hundred and one other delights that would appeal to a Salvationist.*

THE EMPTY CHAIRS

At first, Kenneth McIntyre was just happy to be alive. A Staff Bandman on the *Empress*, he survived with only a few scratches — and then, phoning his father, Colonel McIntyre of New York, he was asked, "Son, if I arrange passage on the next steamer, will you come?"

That he did, travelling to New York and thence by another liner to the Congress. A Staff Band scarlet uniform was sent along for him to wear.

Before departure, McIntyre told a dramatic story to the New York *Herald*. No lifebelts being at hand, he gave his own to a woman without one, and slipped into water "thick with human beings clamoring for life." He found himself going in circles and then remembered a chat, just hours before, about astronomy. "I looked up and fixed two stars," he said. "They were to be my guide."

In London's Strand Hall on June 15, a special Canadian Session day, 133 empty seats were overlaid with white sashes bearing crimson crowns, to symbolize victory, with cards naming each Salvationist thus "promoted to glory" in lieu of attending.

Where the Staff Band would have been, Kenneth McIntyre sat alone amid those draped empty chairs.

Then he was called upon to speak. He simply repeated the 46th Psalm, this having been read at the Staff Band's farewell meeting ten days earlier:

> *God is our refuge and strength, a very present help in trouble.*
> *Therefore will we not fear, though the earth be removed, and*
> *though the mountains be carried into the midst of the sea.*

SOMEWHERE IN FRANCE

A EUROSTAR TRAIN ZOOMS BELOW the English Channel to deposit me at "Lille Europe." My ticket to Paris, bought here, bears two prices — 260.00 Francs, 39.94 Euro: a new continental spirit mutes the nationalism that brought on World War I.

My father was 17 when he contemplated service. "Wilfred and I are the only eligibles to fight of all our Creighton family," he said in a 1915 letter, "and I think it is the duty of one to uphold our good name." On January 22, 1916, soon after turning 18, he sailed from Halifax with the motor transport corps.

What were the deeper effects of combat upon Will, the *Empress* orphan who went to war? I am here to trace his footsteps. Photocopies of his letters and old photos — notably one of himself among fellow truckers taken one sunny day in Tournai, Belgium — are in my pocket. He is shown standing below the N in *restaurant;* with luck I might find the very spot where this was taken.

Now, speeding across northern France by TGV, I view heavy

Will Creighton with other drivers in Tournai, Belgium, 1918 or 1919.

commercial traffic on the adjacent highway — motor transport, my father's wartime calling. Sleek eighteen-wheelers bear high-velocity symbols — rockets, kangaroos, racehorses, arrows, initials coiled into superhighway forms — and logos of brilliant design showing a transcontinental scope: EURO, INTERMARCHE, METRO, NOR-CARGO, INTERNATIONAL, TRANS.

The trucks of Will Creighton's day, on roads often deep in mud, barely surpassed horse-and-wagon efficiency levels.

In 1917, the war's darkest year, Will suddenly stopped writing letters. "No, this is not an obituary notice," he said when correspondence to sister Edith resumed on August 2. It was his first message since March — "so long ago that I've completely forgotten how to make a letter and how to spell." Still a teenager, he had become exhausted by war.

Supplying ammunition, then collecting the dead: this was Will's vocation. It was murder on the grand scale, *promotion to glory* a forgotten dream.

Writing on November 11, 1917, Will told of "trying my hardest to try to think of something to say but it is one hard job." This was five days after a hard-won victory at Passchendaele, where rains flooded shell-torn earth to create a six-mile-wide quagmire; even cannons would disappear into it, yet roads had to be constantly rebuilt for the trucks he drove. Passchendaele was described by Winston Churchill as "a forlorn expenditure of valour and life without equal in futility."

My ticket is printed with a transit time of only one hour. I check this with the white-haired conductor, who smiles proudly and writes "300 km" on the back: that's the distance, that's the speed. These trains, defeating even the Channel on their *grand-vitesse* paths, are a wonder of the age.

Paris: lovers intertwined in the cafés. Will was here twice during the war. The men in his unit all took turns getting passes for their first visit; drawing lots for a second time around, he was the first to go. "I never drank after that," he later recalled: something happened on that second Paris visit, enough to make him mend his ways.

A 1919 photo shows Will aboard ship, with something that looks very much like a *cigarette* in his mouth — although in boyhood I dismissed this as a flaw in the photo. Never could he have smoked, never could he have defiled the "temple of his body"! Finally he admitted that yes, during those years he had "done everything his buddies did."

Three years later, a woman changed my father's life. The key letter is one with a letterhead reading "Mount Royal Hotel / Banff, Alberta" and signed with the name "Maréchale." This was another of William Booth's evangelist daughters, Kate, who claimed French soil for the Salvation Army here in 1881, despite a series of near-riots.

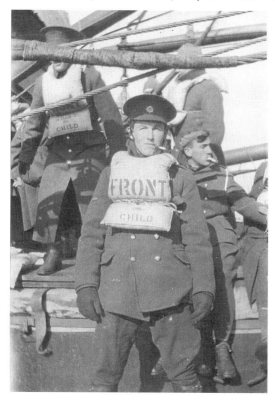

Will sailing home, 1919.

Kate Booth's eyes would glow when she preached, boring into those of every listener. She was therefore known as the "heavenly witch," *la sorcière céleste.* Her troops also awarded her the title of *maréchale,* marshall.

The heavenly witch was 23 in 1881, and had reached her early sixties when Will heard her preach. That was in Calgary where, as one biography states, "the Methodist church was packed full with people sitting on the windowsills. Men's meetings were attended by over 2000. 'She is the most wonderful woman preacher in the world,' they said."

Kate Booth, it seems, was the one who brought my father back into the Christian fold. And off the boulevard de Belleville today I find an unwed-mothers residence named after her. Perhaps it was here that the Maréchale, working with two other young Englishwomen and speaking broken French, endured attacks that led the *gendarmes* to close their hall for six weeks.

"My dear son in the Gospel," wrote the Maréchale to my father. "Surely the Blessed Child Jesus put it into your heart to send those beautiful flowers to cheer me!" Very much unlike the customary Protestant wording, of course — a fact explained by her habit of adapting Catholic procedure to win souls.

In her loft above the hall she would hear confessions — the "Cure of Souls" — and there was always a lineup of those wishing to unburden their hearts. When a Protestant woman decried this practice, the Maréchale chided her for narrowness and added, "Our Lady would like it if you prayed to her Son."

For more about *la sorcière céleste*, I am told to visit the Paris headquarters, at 60 Frères Flavien. Here I am introduced to Captain Patrick Booth, great-great-grandnephew to the Maréchale. He shows me an illustration of Kate preaching in a Paris bistro; she would not hesitate, says the caption, to "uproot her fellow-creatures from the disorders born of alcohol and sloth."

Kate Booth in Paris, early 1880s.

A tale is told of ruffians getting up to dance in her Army premises one night. "Friends, I'll give you twenty minutes to dance, if you will give me twenty minutes to speak!" Kate exclaimed — and this led to the first of a hundred conversions the first year, with some five hundred during the next.

Patrick smiles. "I know that story," he says. We discuss the strange follow-up: Kate leaving the Army to wed a Scot who dreamed of building "Zion City," with a domed temple drawing multitudes to be saved for the Lord. Foundations were laid on a 6500-acre site north of Chicago, before these plans came to grief. "She wanted to stay in the Army, but had to go along with him," Patrick notes.

Invariably her message would be to open one's lips to God, as at Pentecost when the Holy Spirit descended. The letter to my father shows Kate advising him in this spirit: "Listen, you will testify. <u>Fear not.</u> Just rise in simple childlike faith and tell of your Lord — it will come easier every time."

Soul searchings led Will to become a Salvationist, as a Covenant Card signed by him on December 22, 1922 indicates: "I have accepted the Lord Jesus Christ, God's only Son, to be my Saviour." Why did he do so? Because relatives all around him still belonged. And because of the Maréchale — someone in the same age bracket as his lost mother.

As bells ring for 7 p.m. mass, I stroll though *centre-ville* to gare St. Lazare, for a trip to Le Havre. I leave from track 24, on which luxurious boat trains used to depart, each carriage being marked by enameled plaques hanging from the platform side. The restaurant-car manager would ring his bell for table bookings, waiters then serving the courses in platter-to-plate fashion. Not so tonight; passengers nibble on snacks while reading Zola and Stephen King.

Darkness falls, and at Rouen the Flamboyant-Gothic cathedral is only a silhouette. A smell of fresh perfume gathers as women leave the train.

My father's first letter from the continent, "Somewhere in France," was sent to Edith on May 16, 1916. A World War II-era letter sent to his nephew Bill, then also fighting in Europe, makes clear that his arrival point had been Le Havre.

Rouen was a motor transport depot where Will's unit stayed before going to Flanders. Later, moving on to his war-zone base —

an "ammunition park," his task being largely to deliver artillery shells — Will recorded the first casualties in his unit: two wounded and two killed.

My trip continues, in reverse direction to his in 1916. "Coming up on the train it seemed to be a continuous mass of woods and hills," he wrote. "I was very lucky on the train, getting into a second class coach with nice cushions, as some of the boys were in third class while other British Tommies were in box cars."

Le Havre's station boasts a bronze relief of rails supporting an anchor flanked by nymphs hoisting a load of fruit — this having long been a major train/ship juncture. Outside is a lineup of *moulles* eateries and cheap hotels. The Hôtel d'Yport, flashing a neon two-star welcome, receives me for my first night in Europe.

Jean-Paul Sartre, a high school teacher like myself, had a station-area room fictionalized as that of Antoine Roquentin in his 1938 novel, *Nausea*. "From my window," says Antoine, "I see the red and white flame of the 'Railwayman's Rendezvous' at the corner of the Boulevard Victor-Noir. The Paris train has just come in."

Will passed through Le Havre just before hearing from Grandfather William. "As I feel you must be in a dangerous place and a cruel place, I am thinking of you every day and praying you shall be kept safe," he wrote, adding a wish that "the good spirit of God" would prevail.

But Soldier Will's letters give no mention of God. His paybook listing for religion reads "Presbyterian"; he seems to have forsworn the clan's evangelistic faith.

I head downtown to find the square St. Roch and search, in vain, for any sign of the famed chestnut tree whose roots grip the earth under Roquentin's bench — manifesting the fact of existence, as stated memorably in *Nausea*:

> *If anyone had asked me what existence was, I would have answered, in good faith, that it was nothing, simply an empty form which was added to external things without changing anything in their nature. And then all of a sudden, there it was, clear as day: existence had suddenly unveiled itself. It had lost the harmless look of an abstract category: it was the very paste of things, this root was kneaded into existence.*

Nearby is the former Guillaume Tell, where Sartre regularly ate *choucroute*. Simone de Beauvoir took pleasure in its "red plush banquettes and plate-glass bay windows." It has been made over into the Restaurant La Boucherie, with portraits of cattle as human beings — Mme. Vache uses a cigarette holder — and a hollowed-out cow's bone, *os à moelle*, to hold the bill.

Young Annette, my server, leans on a railing to contemplate her foreign guest. Where do I come from? she asks. Why don't I eat more? Am I some kind of writer? In turn I ask what writing Annette does, and she makes a face. How ridiculous!

Yet as an English teacher, this is what I had my students do, exploring life in words, and Sartre required the same here in Le Havre. I walk over to the Lycée Francois I, on a street now named after Sartre. Here he taught, and once gave a Prize Day speech that scandalized parents by praising the cinema, then viewed with suspicion (as also by Salvationists guarding my soul): "Who will teach you about the beauty of the world you live in, the poetry of speed, machines, and the inhuman and splendid inevitability of industry? Who, if not your art, the motion picture."

The introduction to my paperback copy of *Nausea*, with its grainy cover photo of a man squinting into the sun, summarizes postwar Existentialist clichés: "life re-emerging in the cafés of the Left Bank . . . blackstockinged, makeupless girls . . . responding to the emergency of life in the modern world . . . a thread that winds, seldom dominant but always present, through the central European tradition . . . the same profound concern for the fate of the individual person . . . to Existentialism Sartre has contributed a classically brilliant French mind . . . the idea of freedom became Sartre's main theme . . . ."

In my early twenties, this world view claimed my notice. Like Will, and like my grandfather before him, I underwent a form of conversion.

Existentialism was about being *engagé*: involved, committed, living on the edge. Sartre, who systematized his ideas in a work called *Being and Nothingness*, offered me something that Salvationism seemed not to provide: a view of the real world.

Le Havre, during the war that started one year after *Nausea*'s publication, became the most heavily damaged of all of Western Europe harbours. From *being* to *nothingness*: turned into a cemetery for ships of all kinds; and filled with the wreckage of drydocks, quays, warehouses, repair yards. In place General de Gaulle stands a monument to those who died in the carnage; there are around 60,000 names.

In 1916 when my father began his continental war experience in Le Havre, he used a letter form reducing communication to its basics, and shaving his existence to the minimum:

NOTHING is to be written on this side except the date and signature of the sender. Sentences not required may be erased. If anything else is added the post card will be destroyed.

I am quite well.

I have been admitted into hospital

{ sick } and am going on well.
{ wounded } and hope to be discharged soon.

I am being sent down to the base.

I have received your { letter dated
{ telegram „
{ parcel „

Letter follows at first opportunity.

I have received no letter from you

{ lately.
{ for a long time.

Signature
only. } Will

Date: Aug 14/16

[Postage must be prepaid on any letter or post card addressed to the sender of this card.]

(93871) Wt. W3497-293 4,500m. 7/16 J. J. K. & Co., Ltd.

Postcard from Will to Edith, 1916.

When Will first entered Le Havre after the voyage from England, among the many ships he spotted the *Storstad*. That very ship: repaired, pressed into service — and soon to be torpedoed, joining the *Empress* in a vast array of broken machinery.

What could have been his emotions, to see the boat that had changed everything? To me, he mentioned dockside barrels in Le Havre holding boiled eggs, which he and his fellow-soldiers merrily hurled at one another. Something humorous.

Visiting the port next morning, I view another stream of eighteen-wheelers: GLOBETROTTER, SOUTHERN TRANSPORT, SPANISH CONNEXION. "P&O Ferries," says a sign: the old Peninsular & Orient. And here is the *Pride of Portsmouth*, lit up like a Vegas hotel. Several caravans are about to go aboard. "P&O — now it's a big transport firm, container ships going all over the world," an English vacationer explains. "It will be mainly trucks, this time of year."

The P&O's electronic sign advertises "day club cabins," and I ask about this at the P&O desk. "They give you a base, lock it up and walk around the ship," I am told. "We call this a cruise ferry, it's quite popular." So this is what serves in place of Le Havre's great *transatlantique* liners.

Lonely now beside a pier is a sculpture, *Le Génie de la Mer,* from the hand of one François Carlo Sarrabezolles. It was executed, I find, *pour le Paquebot NORMANDIE 1935.* A fig-leafed young merman, gazing out to sea, holds a trident and cornucopia aloft, as three dolphins dive among the coils of his tail. Here is that Art Deco style whose variants sprang up across the Western world between wars, from Nuremberg to New York.

At the Buffet du Havre, I have my croissant beneath a splendid poster of the *Normandie* at dockside, her three broad funnels painted red and black. A streamlined locomotive, parked alongside, sends a thin smoke plume up toward the cumulus clouds. *PARIS, HAVRE, NEW YORK,* reads the message.

The waitress, a faded blonde with lovely posture, empathizes with me over those lost liners. *"La belle époque, les belles années — malheureusement,"* she murmurs, and offers a small Buffet de Havre brochure portraying that steamer/steam-engine tandem within a rondel evoking sunset.

Brasserie brochure, Le Havre.

THE SHOCK OF THE SHIPS

STAFF BANDSMAN WILLIE WAKEFIELD, lost on the *Empress*, was deeply mourned as an only child. Yet his father perceived the grace of God in this fate: "He hath delivered the righteous from the evil that is to come" — that is, from World War I. Young Wakefield had been spared an even sorrier death, in the trenches.

When the *Empress* disaster's anniversary was kept in 1915, the *War Cry* struck a soul-searching note: "The disaster was interpreted by many as a loud warning to avoid the rocks of formalism and materialism." Had a false direction been taken by the Army? And did God therefore sweep away the *Empress* in anger?

Then the shipwreck, a collision of one great machine on another, passed from memory amid World War I's mechanized slaughter on a colossal scale. By 1916 the *War Cry* commemoration was being phrased in battlefield terms:

> *No cannonading or warlike preparations marked the coming of death to those on the* Empress of Ireland. *Like a bolt from the blue came the shock of the ships, and in a short time — they were not. We live not in the radius of shot and shell and bayonet charge, but we are ever in the zone of death. Readers, let us see to it that we are prepared to die.*

LIKE CORDWOOD

M Y FATHER KEPT HIS World War I khaki uniform and tin hat in our basement, near the coal furnace. Allowing me to wear the helmet in make-believe combat with like-minded boys, he seemed to condone the imperative to defend what must be defended. All day long we would play war, killing and dying at mock fortifications throughout the neighbourhood.

And of course during World War I, 450 miles of trenches stretched from Belgium to the Alps, with combat going on senselessly month after month.

Will's letter dated May 1, 1918 tells of peanut butter received from Edith and shared with Will's mate: "He had to ask what it was as he could not remember the taste of it." This was when Germany, able to concentrate troops on the Western Front after Russia left the war, captured a vast area of France and seemed about to win the war — until foiled by a counter-blow to which my father made a key contribution.

Within a few cliffhanger weeks, it all turned around. And a book illuminating Will's later war experience, the *Short Memoirs* of his motor-transport company in the Third Division, gives an idea of his tasks during 1918:

> *Before Amiens, Cambrai, Valenciennes and Mons, drivers were sometimes compelled to work thirty-six hours at a time, hauling supplies, ammunition and troops for the important operations then under way. As the advance grew, shell holes and mine craters made the roads almost impassible.*

The key operation came near Amiens on August 8, 1918 — later called by Erich Ludendorff, Germany's chief of staff, the "black day" in his army's history. And it was four Canadian divisions, attacking in the centre between other Allied troops, that spearheaded decisive victory.

I take a Paris-Amiens train, on the very line that the Allies' August 8 offensive was meant to liberate. Most of the passengers are men. A couple of Americans have come to see the cathedral. As all stand to get off at Amiens, there is a general beeping of cellphones.

Before August 8, 1918, everything unfolded in absolute secrecy. Amiens was evacuated, to eliminate telephone contact and any likelihood of spying. A message was pasted into every soldier's paybook: "Keep Your Mouth Shut." And this deception scheme, enhanced by signallers' dummy messages, worked to perfection.

A huge force gathered. Augmenting 1,606 French artillery pieces were 2,070 British guns, 646 of them Canadian. There were 530 British tanks and 70 on the French side — crude early models with slow speeds, but in the largest number assembled for one battle during the entire war.

I walk to the cathedral, which has several memorials to the dead of *la guerre 1914-1918*. Those of the Royal Canadian Dragoons, says one, "gave up their lives for the cause of right and liberty during the Great War." A prolonged organ riff in a minor key seems attuned to garish stained-glass hues dappling the stone floors.

On August 8, the most vivid moment came when the Dragoons and two other mounted brigades manoeuvered for the attack. Cavalry: after years of trench stalemate, a combat dream was now to be realized. Colonel W. W. Murray of the 2nd Canadian Batallion, a crack Third Division unit, recalled their assault on Beaucourt-en-Santerre, fifteen miles southeast of Amiens:

> *Above the dust-cloud rose the glitter of lances, their bright pennons flying in the wind, the sheen of the weapons radiating flashes in the sunlight. Cheering wildly, a never-ending line of dragoons, hussars and lancers, galloped over the crossings of the Luce, mounted the slopes on the other side, and swept in a thunder of hoofs through the advanced lines of infantry. With a clear sweep and heedless of the fire that rained upon them, they breasted the face of the hills and disappeared into the blue.*

Easy targets, in the age of industrial war. My father mentioned only the aftermath of that cavalry surge, virtually the last to be seen in modern combat. He helped to collect the bodies of the dead: "Cordwood, just like cordwood."

Brian, here from Norfolk with two friends for a battlefield tour, tells me that only a couple of other cavalry attacks occurred in the entire war: "They would last only two or three minutes. Every horse would be killed."

Brian has read 3,500 books about World War I. Acquaintances assume that he leads a sad life and yet, he states, it is inspiring to learn what men can endure. His father was wounded at Passchendaele: the site could be located to within two hundred feet. How did it feel to stand on the spot? "Eerie, like I'd already been there."

I bring out the photocopy showing my own father in Transport Section No. 4 at Tournai, end of 1918. "Saucy fellow," Brian remarks. "I should expect he would be a lad with the ladies."

Will's cap is at a rakish tilt. His eyes are like his mother's, and mine: slanted, with arching eyebrows. He is slender, eager, almost jaunty — 21, and overseas for the fourth straight year.

Will in Tournai, 1918 or 1919.

At the tourist office I receive an area map. Two ancient Roman roads diverge eastward from Amiens across the Santerre plateau — N29 running through Villers-Bretonneaux, where Australian forces gathered; and D934 to the southeast, where the Third Division attacked along the Canadian Corps' right flank.

A *Short Memoirs* map shows that the rail depot used by the Third Division's trucks — my father's — was Saleux, just south of Amiens. Two dates are given alongside: 31-7-18 and 4-8-18. Some 100,000 Canadian troops were moved fifty miles by rail from Flanders to the Amiens area, then either marched to the front or were conveyed by motor transport.

For my own conveyance, I rent a bicycle from two teenagers in front of the rail station. It has two *accessoires remises*: a *panier avant*, front basket; and an *antivol*, lock. Departing at *heure 14h15* on Vélo No 63, I barely avoid running into another patron before heading toward the hills.

Will transported some of the 291,000 shells allotted to the Canadians. Endless convoys would move during the night and then, vampire-like, halt at dawn. To reduce noise, the trucks' wheels were wound with sacking or rope, and roadways were sanded down. Bombers flew constantly overhead to further muffle the sound.

A six-mile march by the 2nd Batallion late on August 7, says Colonel Murray, took the men "through the straggling town of Boves." By the time I reach Boves I am thirsty enough for several bottles of water, bought from beautiful Lucille at the grocery store. I ask where Boves Wood might be — one of several places of concealment for weaponry — and Lucille points westward, adding that this is now mostly suburbs.

Off I go again, arriving soon at D934 — the Third Division's line of advance, against German troops numerously entrenched to the east — with Gentelles Wood visible beyond. Entering this forest was "a revelation," Colonel Murray states:

> *Carefully camouflaged in well constructed gun-pits, innumerable howitzers were emplaced in clustering groups; tons of shells lay hidden beneath heaps of brushwood; small arms ammunition, bombs and engineering material of all kinds were concealed in huge dumps among the trees. Most interesting of all were the tanks. These monsters were parked in the dark recesses, surrounded at all times by inquisitive infantrymen. Some batallion personnel had been detailed for liaison duty with tank units, and accompanied them through the whole operations.*

"Liaison" is the key word here, for close cooperation in sudden attack would spell victory. It was a foretaste of what later was called *Blitzkrieg*, lightning-war. And the Third Division had the most tanks — thirty-six, as against twenty-one with the first and seventeen with the second.

Crossing D934, I gear down to climb the broad slope crowned by Gentelles Wood. When August 8 came at last the code word,

"Llandovery Castle" — referring to a hospital ship recently torpedoed with only twenty-four survivors — was flashed by each division as it reached the white tape marking jumping-off points. The Third Division was the last to do so, arriving only twenty minutes before zero hour.

"The stillness of the night seemed to intensify the almost inaudible tramp of the attacking troops as they flitted to their assembly areas," Murray writes. "From Gentelles Wood came the dull throb of the tanks as they 'tuned-up' for their journey forward." A few Germans gave reports of their sound, but these were dismissed by higher staff as the product of overwrought nerves.

Watches ticked down to the awaited moment, 4:20 a.m. The din of those 3,676 guns began — "like a colony of giants slamming iron doors as fast as they could go" to one observer — in a creeping barrage, with hundred-yard lifts every few minutes. Then through dense fog, by compass bearing, the platoons advanced.

Surprise was total. What easily ranks as the Allies' biggest victory of World War I had begun.

"We have reached the limits of our capacity," said Kaiser Wilhelm two days later, on learning the full scale of what an official account called *Die Katastrophe*. "The war must be ended."

The dead were given rest near where they fell, mainly in rural graveyards. In the hamlet of Gentelles I find one with the simple rounded-off gravestones of Canadians. Their 3,868 casualties on August 8, including 1,038 dead, were relatively light in the context of that unprecedented triumph.

"The mist clearing, the spectacle of a lifetime was unveiled," Murray writes: "Topping the long rolling hills, wave upon wave of Canadian infantry were sweeping irresistably forward, driving before them groups of Germans."

Pedalling south from Gentelles, I distantly view a meandering valley made by the "low, sluggish and swampy" Luce River. On its north bank by the much-fought-over ruins of Hangard, two men earned Victoria Crosses, one posthumously.

By the afternoon of August 8, Murray noted, battle turmoil became a memory: "The crash and smother of the artillery had given way to a profound silence, and unsightly trench systems to deep, shaded valleys which somehow refused to admit the riot of war. The waters of the Luce rippled lazily below overhanging willows, cool and inviting in the intense heat."

My own effort this afternoon produces a thirst to be quenched in Boves once more. Lucille, amused as I empty bottle after bottle, becomes curious about my travels. I tell her about *les batailles de la Grande Guerre*, and she replies in melodious French. We are alone in the store. I think about my father, who might well have been "a lad with the ladies" in these foreign parts offering opportunities galore.

Yet all we know is what Will writes to Edith. Parcels were sent to him by women such as an otherwise-unknown Marion, who enclosed one stick of gum "and asked me that when I was chewing it to think of her. I nearly had a fit, laughing." Some wrote "lonely soldier stuff" — notably a Miss Ezard, who sent her photo in one parcel: "She isn't bad looking but I'll swear she is about sweet sixteen, twice and is about six foot two."

Taking a slow train back to Lille, I gain a view of the Australian memorial at Villers-Bretonneaux. It was a brilliant Australian Corps commander, Sir John Monash, who planned the Amiens victory. And the internal combustion engine made it possible, with one "mechanical transport" company provided for each division. Mobility was all-important: at sea, navies had oil-fired battleships swifter than the *Empress* liners.

"As you can guess from the reports in the papers, I have been very busy," Will wrote on August 17. Two months later, he exulted in "the great things the Canadians have been doing; trucks had been "on the road most of the days and nights."

On October 27 he told of civilians newly liberated: "most certainly a delighted bunch after all the bad treatment they have received from the Germans." Two months later, after the November 11 armistice, Will found people in Brussels "absolutely crazy about the Canadian soldiers. One cannot walk along the street without having a whole crowd following."

In Lille I take a room directly opposite the old Flanders station, at the Hotel Continental. Its windows need paint, but open onto a view of the square. All night I hear the fountains. Here is old-style Europe: intimate, noble, well-proportioned, human-scale.

On December 10, Will wrote from Mons: "What seems the best, is to go up town in the evening and see all the stores lit up. They are so much like the stores at home, window dressing etc., that it really makes me quite homesick."

And here tonight, a jumble of neon names is flashing from Le Rallye Café: *FLAMMEKUECHES BAR BRASSERIE CAVE A BIERES BONJOUR WELCOME CAVE BAR NOS MOULES PIZZAS NOS PRESSIONS.*

Occasionally I see young soldiers in camouflage, carrying submachine guns. "You see them everywhere — the station, the métro, the streets," says Jean-Christophe, at the desk. He explains that these are *vigipirates*, trained in anti-terrorist methods.

I visualize troops on these streets in 1918, during the Hundred Days of Allied advance lasting until the November 11 Armistice. Germany, second only to America industrially, now suffered a collapse that can hardly be imagined. "The officers in many places had lost their influence," said Ludendorff, who candidly reported that retiring troops would shout to those entering combat, "You're prolonging the war!"

Corporal Adolf Hitler of the List Regiment, thrown back with the other troops on that Black Day, howled that shirkers had cost them victory. In a bloody fistfight against a recruit claiming that it was stupid to continue the war, Hitler kept swinging until he won — a foretaste of much more brute violence yet to come.

Demoralization took a heavy moral toll. Late in 1918, Will learned from a machine-gun corps sergeant about a Frenchwoman's baby seen with one ear cut off by a German's bayonet. This seems hard to believe, yet not impossible for combat-hardened soldiers facing bitter defeat.

SURREAL

S HELL SHOCK, WHICH PRODUCES quivering and utter withdrawal, struck Will's second driver in 1917. He was taken off the truck, requiring my father to drive alone. With black humour he later told me how this man crazily ran amid shell explosions that, in the deep mud all around, merely went *phhhtttt!*

From World War I sprang Surrealism, art expressing a world gone mad. To run dementedly amid shellbursts is a surreal image. So is that of rich men donning tuxedos to bid farewell on a liner's sloping deck.

On the *Storstad*, eight barely clad *Empress* survivors huddled in the captain's bunk for warmth along with stark-naked Doctor James Grant, rallying himself so that he could attend to countless injuries. Grant would die at 59 from ulcer problems complicated by manic-depression: residual shell shock, one is tempted to say.

Surreal also is entrapment within a huge sinking liner; and *Empress* survivors, like those on the *Titanic*, told of this. Many in Second Class and Third were caught behind gates that kept them from mingling with First Class, said Mr. E. P. Godson. And a First Class passenger, Cedric Gallagher, reported that crew members drove him and his mother from a lifeboat they tried to enter.

Rufus Spooner told about "the frantic women, the struggling men, the cries of those who fell from the sloping deck or tumbled back into the interior of the boat when the stairway leaned." For him it was like a dream. "The head of a woman struck me in the stomach. I couldn't see her, but I knew she was a woman, for the hair floated about me as I grasped at her. I couldn't get a hold and she was swirled away."

Bert Greenaway also remembered calamity as a dream, "played out before grotesque mirrors." While attempting to wrap his sweater around a baby, he was flung down the Empress's deck into the stomach of an elegantly attired gentleman, who shortly swan-dived into the deep and disappeared.

A companionway entered by Bandsman George Wilson was "clogged like a shoal of fish" with desperate people who "surged me up the vertical stairs as though I were toothpaste."

Assistant steward William Hughes, taken down by the plummeting *Empress*, fought off a hysterical girl trying to choke him and surfaced to see an old man whose white beard overspread the beer keg used for support. He reached a nearly filled lifeboat, but was pushed away by a burly man growling, "Go away! No room! No room!" The boat's officer knocked this scoundrel overboard, screaming, so that Hughes could take his place.

Reaching shore and catching the next England-bound boat, Hughes spent a sleepless week coming to terms with what happened: "I asked the liner's chief steward for all his dirty silverware, and I stayed up each night cleaning the silver, as though trying to wash away a secret crime."

OUR LADY OF THE SICK

OR THE *Short Memoirs* of Will Creighton's motor transport corps, group photos were taken in the Walloon city of Tournai, Belgium. Since childhood I have been fascinated by these, especially one with a background of leafless poplars angling back into mist.

As I approach Tournai by train on September 12, it seems inconceivable that much would remain the same. But the old station, with arches of interlocking stone and brick, is fully intact. Gladioli and sunflowers have been artfully placed in backlit alcoves, and the clock is draped with goldenrod.

I step outside — and all is just like in those photos. The poplars have been replanted, but urban textures remain the same. In the one showing Third Division trucks (page 159), the restaurant sign above Will's head has been usurped by one marking a laundromat, *Lavoir de la Gare*. But vehicles are parked at the same angle as before, an Opel Astra 17B in the slot taken by the Daimler beside which he stands.

The photos might have been taken late in 1918, when a million francs were spent for the Third Division's Christmas dinner. Will and his crew missed the feast because their truck broke down, but a woman cooked up some beefsteak, "and she has treated us like a mother."

Later his haversack was stolen, with every photo sent by Edith since the war's start: "If I could only catch who stole it, I'd break his head or die in the attempt for it is the only thing of value I possess and it was of no earthly use to him."

I soon discover the background for a shot of Transport Section No. 4, showing Will among other youths from Vancouver and Oakville and Verdun, their addresses printed alongside: "CREIGHTON, W H . . . 35, The Maples, Bain Avenue, Toronto." Number 30's doorway could be improved with a little paint, Number 29 has lace curtains in the window; all the stonework is in good trim.

Nos. 29-30 now face a war memorial, visited at this moment by a local man introducing himself as Jean-Jacques Bourdeau. The photos amaze him. I explain that this trip, honouring my father, is something like a pilgrimage of the Middle Ages. His father was also in World War I, wounded by a dum-dum bullet in the back.

Will (top, fifth from left) with his unit in Tournai, 1918 or 1919.

Jean-Jacques fought in George Patton's Third Army during 1944-5, and once saw the general pass by in a tank. "Let's remember all the soldiers," says he abruptly, and we stand silently before the monument. "*Aimez la vie*," he then remarks: enjoy life, that theme expressed by Réal on the *Night Wind*.

For Will, motor transport work intensified after the Armistice. "Civilian rations were hauled," we read in *Short Memoirs*. "Evacuees were returned to their homes in the fought-over district. War materials had to be salvaged and hauled to dumps and railheads."

The men sailed home on the *Scotia* after being demobilized at Tournai. A *DESCRIPTION OF THIS SOLDIER* on the discharge certificate for May 16, 1919 reads:

> Age 21 years
> Height 5'8"
> Complexion Fair
> Eyes Brown
> Hair Red
> Marks or Scars NIL

I have carbon copies of several letters sent by Will to his Army chums, over a long span of time. One, written in 1964 to a man living in Iran, expresses "a lot of nostalgia for those wonderful years."

It reports that Private Ernie Cunningham, seen on Will's right, had died of a severe electrical shock. He names several others who had passed away: "The list is growing and I think it is a good place to stop before we are both too depressed."

The letter betrays an earlier bent towards carousal. In San Francisco Will had found Scotty Ogg (second from the right, sitting down) "cutting up like a two year old" after remarrying in his late seventies: "It's fortunate I am on the wagon, for this reunion put him in a mood to celebrate in the grand style."

I remember Will in solemn moments repeating a phrase used by his mother to describe those we meet during life: "ships that pass in the night." In boyhood I would always visualize her on that ocean liner, not quite able to pass another in the foggy night.

There is a moment in Cameron's *Titanic* when footloose Jack Dawson, caught up in disaster, speaks of freedom even as freezing ocean waters take his life. Be yourself, he tells Young Rose, don't let others set the agenda.

David and Bertha Creighton also sent messages to the living. Fight the good fight. Carry the Army's banner onwards. Save souls for the Kingdom. Earn a victorious crown in paradise. Inspiring: moral focus, a solid link with generations gone before. But also heavy to bear.

Yes, my father had kicked over the traces. Cardplaying, dancing, the demon rum, perhaps even fornication (those trucks so convenient for *les mademoiselles*). His renewed Salvationist ties were still in the future.

Thin altocumulus floats in the sky. A soft breeze comes up as bells of the great Romanesque cathedral begin to ring, and I go there for the 10 a.m. mass. Beside me sits a young mother whose blond child keeps playing with her necklace and embracing her. Incense smoke ascends into the central tower. The choir sings Josef Haydn's *Missa Brevis Sanctis Joannis De Deo*: overwhelming beauty and tenderness.

Would my father have witnessed such glories here, at the end of a war that had spared his life? Salvationism's thrust is to update everything, and thus reach the modern mind — robes and saints and sacraments discarded, allowing faith to connect with the *Zeitgeist*.

When the priests prepare the table, the singing becomes jubilant, almost bouncy. Salvationists abandoned the Eucharist, or

Lord's Supper, largely because the mere flavour of wine holds peril for a recovering alcoholic.

Anyway, they believe, this and the other sacraments are merely outward signs of a spiritual experience that is within, and should never be lost sight of. Every saved person becomes a "priest unto God," and knows the Real Presence in becoming ever more Christlike through genuinely loving action. They grasp what is seen as a deeper spiritual force.

When the choir descends from its loft before a fine rose window, I go up with others to see the organist perform Bach's *Prelude in C Minor*. At the end, all applaud him with big smiles.

Yet Salvationists have instrumental music of their own, and I remember Will's sensitivity to timbre and harmony. During the war, as victory revitalized life on the front, he wrote about the music around him. "We have a miniature orchestra composed of a banjo and violin but our list of songs is about four years old," said he, asking Edith for "the latest ragtime music" in song-sheet form. "Everybody joins in and what the music lacks in quality it most certainly makes up in quantity."

Reading these letters, I try to peer over Will's shoulder into the real world of soldiery. "What a job it is to write," he says, above the din of men "who have just left the estaminet (beer garden) and who are lifting their voices on high." I conjecture the words:

> *When this bloody war is over,*
> *Oh how happy I will be!*
> *No more pork and beans for breakfast,*
> *No more bully beef for tea.*

In Vietnam, GIs had tape-cassette accompaniment by the Doors; during Will's day, soldiers made music of their own. "There is a fine piano player playing," he once wrote, "and every time he starts I can't for the life of me write as I like to hear him so."

Afterwards Will would be keen for music wafted on the airwaves, into radios. A 1922 photo shows my father beside the Model T in which he and a companion drove to the west coast: planks extending from the front to the back seats formed a bed that permitted (in Will's phrase) an occasional "forty winks"; also theirs was the latest in media technology:

8.35 Stopped for Radio Concert. Some job. Hitched wire to phone poles of deserted farm heard Caruso & orchestra, When you and I were young Maggie.

Will on trip to west coast, 1922.

By design I have arrived on the second Sunday in September — the date, ever since 1092, of a procession expressing thanks to the Virgin for saving the city from pestilence. It is the biggest annual rite held in any Walloon city.

At 2:55 p.m. on the main square a carousel whirls, a fountain spasmodically spurts, *Only the Lonely* blares from a bar window, children ride little sailboats on an afternoon called the Surf. Then at three, modernity gives way to a scene from the Middle Ages, as *La Grand Procession de Tournai* begins.

The Theban Trumpets, in black with coloured ribbons down to their ankles, give a fanfare. Three heralds ride on horseback into the square, accompanying churchmen in all their finery. Two matronly women in black velvet bear a sign between them: *In the year 1090 Tournai was ravaged by plague. Our Lady of the Sick delivered the city from that curse.*

The Royal Brass Band of the Voluntary Fire Brigade of Tournai plays a solemn tune. Brass and drum: Salvationist-style music in a heartland of Catholic symbol and sacrament.

And now, the processional cross. "Looking at the image of the cross," says the illustrated guide to these rites, "a Christian remembers Jesus Christ who suffered on the cross to save all people." Strange flower-bedecked items appear next: silver reliquary arms, holding relics of two revered saints.

Medieval piety manifests itself with gorgeous costumes out of a Jan van Eyck painting. The devout, in rich greens and scarlets and blues and vermilions and burgundies and blacks, bear statuary images such as Protestantism abhors. Only in 1566, when iconoclasts held the city, did the Grand Procession not occur.

Opposite the carousel a churchman delivers commentary — slowly, with adoration, in sorrowful tones — at the arrival of each group of marchers. These people with their ancient beliefs, who want only peace, have their brief moment in the sun. Quietness, a rich variety of texture and hue, pure devotion, words resonantly delivered, calm dignity — this faith with roots deep in the past holds an extraordinary spell.

A silver reliquary head with relics of St. Margaret is accompanied by children, only children. All are gowned in white. I am moved by their youth, their sudden brightness amid the city's old stone, their innocence and hope.

La dévotion mariale is next, the marchers' robes and flowers they bear all colour-coded to the image: Our Lady of the Family, Our Lady of Mercy (a baby sucking at Mary's breast), Our Lady of the Golden Heart, Our Lady of Blissful Demise, and many others. Exquisite shrines come next and when that of the Blessed Sacrament appears, at the very end, many fall to their knees in veneration.

Then just after four, even as the Blessed Sacrament is being carried through the square, amusements recommence. "Ladies and gentlemen — the Surf — is about to begin!" says a mechanical voice as those sailboats start to go around and the children within — all except one terrified little boy — seize basketballs to be hurled violently into a central hoop.

THEN WE'LL ANCHOR
IN THE HARBOUR

I N THE ARENA ON Mutual Street, flowers had been banked around a large enclosed box in the shape of a cross. A hundred young Salvationist girls sat nearby, robed in white.

At a designated time, the girls marched from their seats to stand within the cross's low walls. Then voices were raised in an old song, "We are out on the ocean sailing":

> *All the storms will soon be over,*
> *Then we'll anchor in the harbour.*

Profound emotions of pity and release swept through the audience as these voices rose in their faint treble:

> *We have kindred over yonder*
> *On that bright and happy shore;*
> *By and by we'll swell the number*
> *When the toils of life are o'er.*

Salvationist girls in flower-edged cross at *Empress* funeral.
(George Scott Railton Heritage Centre)

WHEN THE PLOT
STARTS TO DRAG

GOING UP TO EDINBURGH, I enter ancestral ground. In the Castle's Great Hall one finds several Crichtons listed among the palace governors, including two Davids. A family crest in Victorian stained glass cites "Sir William Crichton Chancellor 1438," who ruled Scotland during James II's childhood.

A grisly tale of those times is told by Jim, the guard. "There was bad blood between the king and the Douglasses," he begins. This clan had a thousand men in its army, and posed a threat to young James: "Unknown to the king, treachery was afoot."

The two Douglasses were brought here for a convivial banquet — a "public relations exercise," with only a hundred men accompanying them. Then a black bull's head was brought in, the sign of death, and both lads were beheaded on a charge of treason. James went into shock.

> Edinburgh Castle, town and tower,
> God grant thou sink for sin,
> And that even for the black dinner
> Earl Douglas gat therein.

Should I have any regret about my clan's role in such knavery? Absolutely not, says Jim. "The medieval Scots were a very warring nation, and this was a political decision."

My people, with names ranging from the French-sounding Creton to the very Scottish Creychtoune, had a county seat of Kreiton in Midlothian. It was a border clan, known for never failing to help neighbours recover lost property — and thus the family name could mean "den of thieves"; it is a matter of interpretation. But that Michael Creighton killed a hare in Ulster, riling some indignant landowner, seems conclusive.

Jim offers to explain the expression "half cut." With keen delight he seizes a giant claymore, and makes as if to drive the blade through my skull. "This was used as a deterrent," says he; "slice you right down to the liver — *half cut!*"

At the new Museum of Scotland, among the documentary films continuously shown is *So Many Partings.* Emigration: grief-stricken farewells. One woman is shown waving at the end of a dock to loved ones already far away.

An Ontario man, as moved as I am by the film, tells about a family breaking up before his eyes at Prestwick Airport: "Someone would sing a sad song, and they'd cry; then another sad song, they'd cry again, and so on." Sentiment — the Scots acknowledge and express it.

Scots also built the liners on which many departed, and here is a model of a triple expansion steam engine built by Fairfield Shipbuilding & Engineering. Earlier, under the name of Randolph, Elder and Co., it had patented a revolutionary compound steam engine providing improved range and using 30-40% less coal.

A flamboyant Fairmont head, Sir William Pearce, introduced a high-speed line of transport ships, the "Atlantic Greyhounds." It was he who initiated the Blue Riband award for the fastest time between Britain and New York. The firm also gained repute for warships, building 160 Royal Navy vessels in all.

A grainy 1905 photo shows a thirty-eight-gun battle cruiser built by Fairfield, and here are items presented by the Countess of Dundonald at its launching: a silver casket (with an image of the cruiser in full steam) and a carved wooden hammer.

The armada sent out by Fairfield underpinned the British Empire, and thus it is apt that in 1906 the *Empress of Ireland* slid from its ways.

In Glasgow, I cross the Clyde to visit Govan, a small fishing community until the Fairfield farm was bought in 1864 by a successful marine engineer, John Elder. It became the world's largest private shipyard, employing over four thousand men.

The "Clyde symphony," a harsh metal-bashing tune, was played here by skilled workers throughout two world wars. Then, new global alignments undermined local shipbuilding. Fairfield was acquired by a Norwegian parent company, Kvaerner.

At the Old Govan Arms pub, making known my interest in shipyards, I am introduced to Jim McFall, a Kvaerner crane operator. "Come on, I'll take you through," he says, and I am promptly given a look at the offices, with their fascinating old photos.

Here is one showing construction underway on the *Empress of Japan* — which, after a name change during World War II hostilities, plied the Quebec-Liverpool route. A battle cruiser is moored nearby. The Fairfield yards, circa 1930: a microcosm of that fast-fading empire.

Jim gives a rapid survey of current technique. Huge twenty-eight-wheel vehicles, "shirleys," are used to convey entire prefabricated ship sections from one place to another, allowing most of the work to be done under cover. With gusto he shows me one great unit ready for placement: "That's a complete bridge!"

Several ships are well on the way to completion. "There's No. 319, for oil-well drilling — it processes its own oil!" says Jim. "No. 320, icebreaker; No. 321, auxiliary oiler. We prefer to use numbers, but No. 319 has a name already: *Crystal Ocean.*"

Fairfield once had a mill that could reduce timbers up to forty-two inches in diameter; but there's no more woodwork, only steel. A huge loft was built for the task of cutting templates, now made redundant by computers.

Fairfield yards, 1990s. (Berth 4 behind topmost crane.)

Jim shows three building berths that remain, of the five that once functioned here. "Berth 3 — the red crane!" Jim indicates. "Berth 4, what's left of it — past that white building!"

Berth 4 on January 27, 1906 was the launching-place of Hull 443, the *Empress of Ireland*. "The launch platform, festooned with bunting, was crowded with over 90 dignitaries representing the shipyard and Canadian Pacific," writes David Zeni in *Forgotten Empress*: "The *Empress's* propellers spun a little as she hit the water. The crowd cheered. The tugs and a flotilla of small craft sounded their whistles in tribute."

Five tugboats were required to bring her to the fitting-out basin. Then at a celebratory luncheon, shipyard director Sir Digby Morant proposed a toast: "Success to the *Empress of Ireland* and prosperity to the Canadian Pacific Railway Company."

For Jim, of course, the present is what counts. And somehow, Fairfield survives. He ends on a proud note: "Clyde-built is the best, highest standards in the world!"

One query, about that all-underwater rudder on the *Empress*, sticks on my tongue. Should I mention this, and the long-disputed question of her maneuverability? No, that was too long ago.

My Dublin train ticket, allowing ferry passage to Ireland, has one catch: the boat arrives at 2 a.m. in Belfast, from which the first Dublin train leaves at 7 a.m.. Fine: I'll pass the small hours in some all-night spot. An adventure.

My aim is to re-enact my forebears' seventeenth-century emigration to Irish properties. England, embracing the Reformation, hoped to protect her back door in Catholic Ireland by settling Ulster with those "undertaking" to remain Protestant there. "Undertakers" such as my people accomplished this end, which required the locals to be driven out — and caused discords only now being resolved.

From Belfast Quay at 2:20 a.m. (the ferry a little late) I find my way toward the city centre, briefly reclining on a bench until personal-safety concerns impel me on. I meet only a yellow lab, who scurries away in fear. This kills time until I discover a 24-hour McDonald's, and sit in a corner until the rail station opens.

At home I have loved ones, security, warmth, far more material comforts than I need. So the darkness of soul I experience now is contrived, in a sense. What is homelessness like, when viewed as permanent? Salvationists address such problems.

And in Belfast I find one of the Army's fundraising "Deliver us from evil" billboards: a heroin addict in a bedsit, mainlining. Images for this and other evils targeted — prostitution, poverty, homelessness — are so shocking that three British cities refused display sites.

I continue to Dublin, where I am in the right mood to locate a few Samuel Beckett sites around town. "I shall always be depressed," Beckett told a friend, "but what comforts me is the realization that I can now accept this dark side as the commanding side of my personality." Salvationists, by contrast, believe that God is love and joy lies in the heaven.

In London I visit the Nelson Monument, where wartime photos show my father standing beside one of the lions. His patriotic emotion stemmed from a blood allegiance rooted in the Scottish borderlands, Ulster, and "Great Britain." So a famed Nelson utterance, inscribed here below a scene of his demise at Trafalgar, is one that Will saw fit to obey: *England expects every man will do his duty*.

Just down the Mall stands Buckingham Palace, where in 1914 George V was visited by General Bramwell Booth. "The King received me with great kindness and at once drew me to a chair near his own," said he, adding that the monarch expressed sympathy over the *Empress of Ireland*'s sinking. "The King said he felt it so pathetic that our comrades should be lost when they were on their way to the reunion of our forces at the Congress."

"Did the King mention the dear old General, sir?" asked the *War Cry* correspondent, referring to the late William Booth.

"Yes, he spoke to me in words which were more than those of respect and veneration."

The monarch's good will was also expressed to Will at war's end, in a note received by colonials who had served "a grateful Mother Country."

A highlight of my last day is *The Sinking of the Titanic / A Complete Disaster*, given at the Riverside Studios in Hammersmith. John Fiske, as "Sidney," avidly stages the liner's doom in this "comic catastrophe in rather bad taste." Paul Kessel is the straight man, "Gilbey."

"Gilbey, you can play the captain," says he. "I want you pacing about the deck, the responsibilities are heavy on your shoulders."

BUCKINGHAM PALACE.

The Queen and I wish you God-speed, and a safe return to your homes and dear ones.

A grateful Mother Country is proud of your splendid services characterized by unsurpassed devotion and courage.

George R.I.

George V's goodwill message received by Will.

Gilbey thus is made to learn about Captain Smith's disaster role.

"I get a warning about ice and I do — nothing?" he asks.

"It was just one little mistake — and he *paid* for that mistake!"

"How did that help?"

"It made him a hero! He did what England expected!"

Gilbey, who has a Ukrainian mother, finds it impossible to *appreciate* what Britishness demands. But he learns a moral in the tale: "It signaled the end of the old class system — I got a book out from the library, and it said that that disappeared, never to return!"

Sidney suggests the very opposite, that *Titanic* social divisions foreshadow those of our own day: "If we apply modern free market principles, the owners of those lifeboats would have made a *profit.*"

"But lifeboats should be for all!"

"So what if the first class got them," Sidney replies; "it's like private medicine, this is why people want to be rich!"

When Sidney aspires to total realism in representing death at sea, Gilbey balks: "Babies drowning on stage — I won't do it! It's horrible, it's grotesque!"

Paul Kessel and John Fiske.

"But they died in very large numbers, four figures; we can't let the audience down," he is told. "And when the plot starts to drag, you've got to begin the deaths. That's what makes the *Titanic* such a winner!"

To find the "dramatic truth" in drowning, they put plastic bags on their heads as if to suffocate. "Tell me what it's like afterwards — wait until you are *fighting* for breath," Sidney commands.

The bags are not tight enough, and they just stand there: the funniest moment in the show. A shipwreck drama which, finally, gives the cutting edge of truth.

PART FIVE

MYSTERIOUS CIRCUMSTANCES

DAMNED GOOD SHOW

The goldenrod beside the meadow droops and withers on its stem. The maples blaze in glory and die. The evening closes dark and chill, and in the gloom of the main corner of Mariposa the Salvation Army around a naphtha lamp lift up the confession of their sins — and that is autumn.
        Stephen Leacock,
        Sunshine Sketches of a Little Town

DRIVING INTO THE CANADIAN National Exhibition grounds on Toronto's waterfront, I find everything much the same: Ontario Government Building, fountain, bandshell, Press, Queen Elizabeth Exhibit Hall (royal trappings), Sports Hall of Fame, stadium — *what happened to the stadium?*

"Gone with the wind!" I am told by a passerby, Mike. "Blue Jays were there, Argos — now all that's left is that little thing where rock bands used to play, they moved it up by those temporary stands."

Then what about the Warriors Day parade, once the CNE's climactic event? "I think they march through the midway, end up at the bandshell," says he. "Like, they don't need a whole stadium!"

I mention an uncle, Gordon Dennis, a World War I flyer who gained a bad wound but also the Distinguished Flying Cross. His medal was awarded here at the original Exhibition Stadium two years after the war's end.

"There's only one guy left in the city from World War I, it was in the paper," says Mike. "I used to drive a vanload of vets from Sunnybrook Hospital down here for the parade, leave them by the entrance. The others would march in, eh?"

On the Roman-triumphal Princes' Gate, I find a text about its 1927 opening: "First to pass through these gates was a veterans' parade under the auspices of the Canadian Legion & the British Empire Service League for a review by HRH the Prince of Wales."

On the 1920 Warriors Day, Gordon Dennis was among five airmen — including Billy Bishop, the top Allied ace with seventy-

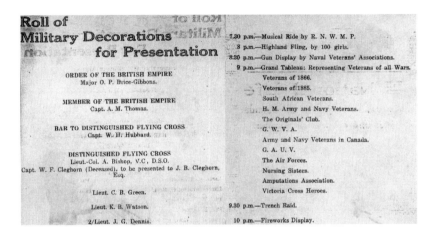

Roll of Military Decorations for Presentation

ORDER OF THE BRITISH EMPIRE
Major O. P. Brice-Gibbons.

MEMBER OF THE BRITISH EMPIRE
Capt. A. M. Thomas.

BAR TO DISTINGUISHED FLYING CROSS
Capt. W. H. Hubbard.

DISTINGUISHED FLYING CROSS
Lieut.-Col. A. Bishop, V.C, D.S.O.
Capt. W. F. Cleghorn (Deceased), to be presented to J. B. Cleghorn, Esq.

Lieut. C. B. Green.

Lieut. K. B. Watson.

2/Lieut. J. G. Dennis.

7.30 p.m.—Musical Ride by R. N. W. M. P.
8 p.m.—Highland Fling, by 100 girls.
8.30 p.m.—Gun Display by Naval Veterans' Associations.
9 p.m.—Grand Tableau: Representing Veterans of all Wars.
Veterans of 1866.
Veterans of 1885.
South African Veterans.
H. M. Army and Navy Veterans.
The Originals' Club.
G. W. V. A.
Army and Navy Veterans in Canada.
G. A. U. V.
The Air Forces.
Nursing Sisters.
Amputations Association.
Victoria Cross Heroes.
9.30 p.m.—Trench Raid.
10 p.m.—Fireworks Display.

Official program for 1920 Warriors Day, Canadian National Exhibition.

two aerial kills reported — to receive medals at the Ex. The official program lists a "Trench Raid" as the culminating show.

Gone with the wind, that war mania. But as fascinating as ever is a certain four-stack liner featured in a Better Living Centre display, *Titanic / The Exhibit*, which promises a look at "personal belongings that poured from the doomed ship."

In the Better Living Centre, dying is the draw today. Here we find the jacket of assistant steward Athol T. Broome, who worked in the Verandah Cafe: the garment, bearing a surname still clearly legible, has survived the person.

"Excellent, sad, and it brought the passengers back to life," someone has written in the visitors' book. Another states, "I am struck by the romance of the age which unfortunately has been lost as we end this century." Says a third, "I couldn't help feeling I was sharing an intimate moment with the passengers and crew members."

One newly penned remark would be of interest to Kessel and Fiske: "I thought it was great because it was a great reminder of a horrible disaster."

I find myself likening the *Titanic* to a brain-weak Triassic life-form, blundering into extinction. Some twentieth-century machines have had good survival instincts — the DC-3 and B-52, the Model T and the Volkswagen — while others have not.

Gordon, piloting a new DH-9 bomber equipped with BHP engines that turned out to be failure-prone, was shot in the bowels on his second mission. He beckoned to the observer to take the controls but the man shook his head, having been hit as well. Blood from his wound flowed forward into Gordon's cockpit as he desperately brought the plane to a safe landing, and immediately collapsed.

Result: a DFC, and discomfort for the rest of his life. The squadron commander was impressed by such determination and, visiting him in the hospital, exclaimed, "Good show, Dennis, damned good show!"

I continue to 145 Front Street East, once housing the J.& J. Taylor Safeworks where Wilfred was long employed. Will also worked here when he enlisted, winning applause from the kindly owner, W. N. West: "You will have some satisfaction for years to come in knowing that you played the game squarely." When Armistice Day came, however, its revelry seemed excessive to this sober patriarch:

> *We had a glorious day here on Monday, the 11th. Rather too hilarious to suit my own personal feelings. The crowds were simply wild, as was only natural, after four years of pent-up emotions.*

At 145 Front, now a medical centre, there were enough younger Creightons working part-time to be a rich source of humour at the firm. This came about through the office-manager prestige of Wilfred — whose high laugh, almost like crying, would often be heard here alongside Will's. We would always know which one had cracked the joke: he who laughed more loudly.

Where the Archer Co-op now stands, the Taylors' foundry operated. I served as a messenger in that pre-pager era, and walking from here back through the plant gave overview of a huge manufacturing process unfolding, almost from scratch. It ended in the paint shop, where an ancient fellow with trembling hands somehow added letters and scrollwork to the finished product.

I remember the heavy labour, the dirt, the long hours. Work continued on Saturday until noon, when many would load up on groceries at the St. Lawrence Market a block away. Then, onto the streetcars for the trip home, in that compact and sinewy town of long ago.

In a building at Yonge and King, once the city's epicentre, young

Letterhead, J. & J. Taylor Safeworks, circa 1915.

Arthur headed the Canadian Pacific's Colonization Department. Will, proud of him for becoming "one of the local leading lights," told about a 1937 Empire Club meeting in Toronto: "Wilf and I were there of course sitting down amongst the common herd, but up on the dais amid all the tycoons and big shots sat our brother Arthur . . . and carrying off the honours in fine style."

Fancy metalwork still guards the entrance ramp at 69 Yonge, and its old name can be discerned in the grime: *Canadian Pacific Building*. The former ticket-sale room now holds a Shoppers Drug Mart, each of the five downstairs aisles being devoted to the human body: first, lips/nails; second and third, hair; fourth, teeth/skin; fifth, stomach (pop, candy).

In a less privileged era, many would have saved up their money to buy *Empress* tickets here for visits to kinfolk in the Old Land. On May 29, 1914 this is where many awaited word about loved ones, as the *World* states: "It was a common sight to see well-dressed women standing in the drenching rain at King and Yonge streets eagerly discussing the chances of some friend on board the wrecked liner."

I continue past the Don River to 136 Hogarth, where David and Bertha lived at the time of their demise. Today it stands behind many tall Rose of Sharon plants. All seems placid and secure this evening, and musical to the ear is a din of children playing in nearby Withrow Park.

Gordon Dennis — the "brave one" in his Cornish family, who emigrated to Canada all by himself at 19 — lived next door. I couldn't say which house was his, but this hardly matters because No. 138 has been entirely resurfaced, and No. 134 is a new building altogether. Edith was going around with a plate of cookies on the night they met, and her beauty made him hesitate. "Well, go ahead!" she laughed.

That he did, undertaking to attend Edith's Salvation Army meetings (at a corps on Chester, long gone) and to walk her home afterwards. She soon responded to Gordon's gentle affection, perhaps in part because she enjoyed zooming around on his motorcycle. A courtship of only 2 1/2 weeks led to engagement — and off he went to war.

Four streets further down is Bain Avenue, where No. 100 is a catch-all address for several English-style "co-ops," as they are now called. These were named after trees — oaks, maples, cedars — which happen to abound today amid the courtyards, though not on a tree-to-co-op basis.

Edith lived with Wilfred in 35, The Maples, when she received those wartime letters from Will. Deeply in love, she once asked for a description of her beau. Will teasingly replied that he had "not spent very much time looking into his lovely eyes," but Gordon "always has a nice little smile for me when we meet."

"Co-ops — everybody works together fixing them up," says Shane at 33, The Maples; "pay mortgages to the government." He enjoys it here: "Small-townish, which is good and bad because people know what you're doing. But very friendly here, talkative — I'm from Nova Scotia, I like it." And the Creightons were also Maritimers; I describe their New Brunswick roots. "Sussex — I've gone through Sussex!"

For Shane I open *Short Memoirs*, to show my father's photo alongside the address: 35, The Maples, Bain Avenue, Toronto. "Cool," Shane remarks.

At the front, Will dwelt longingly on family photos sent by Edith from No. 35. He marvelled at how Cyrus had grown: "quite a boy with his two piece suit, tie and big cap . . . he seems to look a great deal like Arthur used to only more talkative. Am I right?"

He notes how war mania has captivated the boy: "Cyrus says he wishes he was a soldier for he would like to kill the Kaiser, also he wants me to bring home a Zep [German airship] which I'm afraid will be some job."

A letter of May 1, 1918 strikes a new note of tenderness toward Edith, overworked as a secretary at Standard Brick's munitions plant: "Remember we have only got one sister in our family and if she were

View of Bain Avenue from No. 35, The Maples, during World War I.

to get played out we couldn't get another such as her in this whole wide world."

Edith kept a diary, recording deep anxiety about Will and Gordon. On October 5, 1918 she wrote:

> *Received a letter from Ethel saying that Gord had been wounded.*
> *I went over to the Champions and then was in to Mrs. M. &*
> *Miss Scott's. Then I did a lot of walking & wrote to Willie.*

A few blocks away stands 26 Hurndale Avenue, just off the Danforth. Here Gordon and Edith, reunited and newlywed, lived after the war. He hoped to acquire a farm through the Soldiers' Settlement Board — a dream also held by Will, who wrote from Calgary to suggest that they might have adjoining lands out there. Wilfred, also living at No. 26, became alarmed at the likelihood: "If Gordon and Edith move West, I will be alone, which I don't fancy."

From No. 26 Gordon wrote Will a decisive letter, replete with facts and figures: "I evidently would have to spend a year on a farm that is being operated successfully. I have no intentions of leaving Edie for that length of time, farm or no farm." By 1922, when he found land in Ontario, Will had already relinquished the rural dream: he was living in a crude Alberta farmhouse which, during winter, had a dispiriting film of frost on the walls.

On Hurndale, several families sit on verandahs to enjoy this perfect evening. Edith must have had reservations about leaving Toronto to start rural living.

Today this area offers a variety of gourmet-coffee spots, from which I choose Timothy's World News Cafe for a sandwich-and-cappuccino dinner. World News? "One shelf was all newspapers," the manager explains. "Irish, US, you name it — but they cost five bucks each, so we dropped it."

My table sits beneath an original watercolour, "Female Body Builder." Gordon went into farming for the sake of fresh-air toil to speed convalescence: what would a health-conscious age think of that? And of Wilfred and Vi's decision to have their honeymoon at the Dennises' farm?

I revisit Glenmount Park Road in the east end. Here Will found a house at No. 69 after our California years, which lasted until 1936. "There are many, many things that make this a nice place to live, but the constant realization of the remoteness of the family cannot but pull at our heart strings," Will wrote to Wilfred.

His California dream had died two years before. Labour unrest, stemming from New Deal legislation, plagued Will's struggling steamship firm, ultimately absorbed by the Matson Company — which in turn was hobbled by the unions' 1934 shutdown of coastal shipping, then the city's chief source of wealth.

Back to J. & J. Taylor came Will in 1936, as a salesman in northern territories, which meant icy roads. In one rueful message to California friends, he said that "you might see us rolling into Oakland ere the winter snows get too deep." Then for his initial year at J. & J., Will ranked first in dollar sales among all of the travellers. "To make a long story short," as he used to remark, we stayed in Canada.

No. 69's basement held a coal furnace (red and blue flames amid the black lumps) and a cold cupboard, with bushels of apples gradually softening through the Canadian winter. When Will flooded the backyard, neighbourhood kids would come over for shinny.

Now, on a September evening, comes what used to be a magic hour for street games — hide and seek, may-we-cross-the-river, red rover — which went on tumultuously until it was too dark. Nothing like that happens now, as I determine from an in-and-out circuit of many streets. Only once do I spot any children at all, and that is on our former patch of Glenmount, now one-way to speed the traffic flow; its red-brick fabric has been asphalted over.

I remember how playmates' shouts would be heard from afar, messages given one to another. Secret societies abounded. There was the mystery of gathering dusk, of fall fading into winter, of ourselves passing into adulthood. A drama of the neighbourhood psyche kept unfolding.

Down at No. 12 Arthur and his wife Alma raised their large family, permitting a flow of activity between that address and our own. The four young parents themselves had a chance to cavort after a big 1944 snowstorm, as described in one of Will's letters:

> With the absence of the usual motor car noises plus the sound deadening effect of the deep snow there was a silence that seemed artificial. . . Once the sidewalks were shovelled there was an excellent toboggan slide of which the kids took full advantage, and not only the kids. Arthur and Alma, Doris and I, once the night had fallen and our dignity would not be in jeopardy, were also out renewing our youth.

In 1954 Will, finding 69 Glenmount "somewhat cramped for entertaining guests," moved us to 11 Parkview Hill Crescent in East York. Postwar affluence opened up a new life of easy travel to distant lands, and greater freedom.

There is a 1948 photo of my mother that speaks volumes about how our world had changed. She stands before a passenger plane, and is about to visit PEI on her own. Doris also went back to California by herself in 1964, flinging herself into activities with an energy that amazed Will.

"Don't forget this," she wrote to him. "I am free from all responsibilities and housework, also SA activities, and I haven't had to do any driving, pick up people, any grocery shopping, etc., just travelling and seeing the sights. It's a great life and it will be hard to get back to normal again."

Doris Creighton and Trans Canada Air Lines DC-3, 1948.

Arthur's house at No. 12 was bought by David Creighton as an investment. His Immigration Department wage finally justified such purchases — a step up from the poverty of corps-officer years — and Arthur also showed upward mobility. He augmented family income with a kind of chain-letter scheme for selling "Speed Bank Note Cases." Inviting Will to join in the venture, he pointed out, "It doesn't take much time, it's a lot of fun but requires two things — pep and speed."

In Arthur there was a streak of skepticism, and one day he took the huge step of quitting the Army. Willard Brewing, a Sussex friend who rose to become bishop of Canada's Episcopalian Church, had a Toronto congregation which Arthur joined. He would attend service at St. George's twice each Sunday and later, as Canadian attendance levels dropped, would say, "If you don't go to church, there won't be one."

At No. 12 and other Creighton homes, family patterns known since the nineteenth century were kept up. Each Christmas, there were gatherings at which the designated wife would have to prepare the turkey. That Norman Rockwell spirit of a half-century ago is evoked by a letter sent to California relatives by Will, describing a Christmas feast held at No. 12:

> *Little can be heard but the business-like clash of cutlery*
> *intermingled with remote requests of, please pass this and please*

pass that, and now Gord, just another slice of white meat, and here is the pope's nose for Doris . . . and eventually out comes the rack for Wilf to polish off. Wilf by long and assiduous practice is an expert at this. How under the sun we can make room for apple or mince pie I can't imagine, but we do and still have a little room left for grapes and raisins. At last Alma, I believe they are all filled up, so you can sit down for a little nibble yourself and heave a sigh of relief and say that's that for another three years. . . . It was time for Gordon to think of all the chores awaiting him at the farm and it was necessary for them to go home. . . The next event on the calendar, or should I say the first event on the new calendar, was New Years Day at the Farm. Generally all the crowd go.

Arthur, settling New Canadians for the CPR, would often warn them against the grandiose dreams by which many are led off track. But no collapsing dream world could ever match that of Her Imperial Highness Grand Duchess Olga Alexandrovna of Russia — the full name as rendered on her enormous grave in York Cemetery, behind the Ford Centre in North York.

Olga's brother was Nicholas II, absolute ruler over 133 million subjects until the Revolution. It caused his death whereas she survived, coming to Canada through a process largely arranged by Arthur. For the Grand Duchess he found modest homes, near Campbellville and later Cooksville, for her final exile.

Historian Modris Eksteins sees one major story in our century: not the computer or atomic bomb but human migration, a vast upheaval such as Olga's flight shows in miniature — and usually toward lands where liberal-democratic rights and opportunities are to be found.

Grand Duchess Olga gave to Arthur, her "guardian angel," a water-colour as a Christmas greeting in 1955. "This is my garden & the thing seated there is supposed to be me!!" she wrote. "The top of our Chinese Elm was broken off by the wind — such a pity . . . ."

The war that led to the bloody death of Czar Nicholas and his beautiful family, the war in which Gordon and Will fought, served largely imperial aims. And monarchies in Russia, Germany, and Austria collapsed. For World War I signalled the fall of many earls and landgraves and lords and emperors and kings; of duchesses and archduchesses and viscountesses and marchionesses and empresses.

Grand Duchess Olga, watercolour self-portrait, 1955.

After J. & J. Taylor succumbed to foreign competition, merging with the US-based Mosler company, Wilfred bought a five-acre farm in the rural village of Milliken. He and Vi, his wife, here raised a flock of sheep. "Sometimes the mother would neglect her lambs," she recalled; "I'd keep them in a cardboard box and feed them their bottle by night."

Those five acres at Kennedy Road and Steeles Avenue are now occupied by Pacific Mall, a monolith holding three hundred glass-fronted indoor shops. I am the only Anglo on the premises. Here my uncle, enjoyed the life of a country squire with his nine sheep and numerous hens.

"I've lived around here for a long time and I'll tell you, it's changed," says the security guard. "A big barn used to be here but they tore it down, couldn't make money." He refers to the mammoth Cullan Barns, assembled in Frankenstein fashion from dead normal-sized barns — dragged here after my uncle's departure, and then in turn displaced.

Wilfred was often visited here by Arthur, who became a travel agent in later life. He needed only to rent a church basement, show some slides, and sign up fifty people to a tour. "This is the greatest thing that ever happened to these people," Arthur would say. He did everything with a flair, having them don the Red Tape signifying a kind of knightly order — a united force that would cut through bureaucratic muddle.

Arthur not only took up his father's calling, but embodied the showmanship that David must have shown in the Army. A repertoire of hot-Gospel antics was used, in a sense, to stir up business. "There was a touch of the rascal about him," son Robert says of Arthur. "He always had something up his sleeve."

A tour-group photo, taken in England's Lake District, shows Arthur at left (with camera) and Wilfred at right. "What a lot has been crowded into the time," wrote Wilfred. "This is a fine tour."

Arthur Creighton (left) and Wilfred Creighton (right) with tour group in England, 1950s.

I continue to Scarborough corps, at Warden and Lawrence, where Will was a soldier at the time of his sudden death, in 1971. He was the first of the longer-lived orphans to go. At the funeral home, we could hear his siblings in the adjoining room. Wilfred's voice arose in that laugh of his, like a sob, and this aroused a titter among ourselves. Too bad Will's own laugh didn't chime in.

Then the three survivors emerged into view with the casket, and we could see how far their own physical ruin had advanced. The story of the *Empress* Creightons, its central narrative at least, was quickly drawing to an end. A heart condition ended Arthur's life in 1973, and Wilfred met a similar end two years later.

In Agincourt, I drop in on my brother Fred. In youth he had ventured on an ocean liner to attend another London congress of the Salvation Army and, as if to reverse his grandparents' tragedy, safely arrived and also linked up with the woman he would soon marry: Lieutenant June Owen.

I ask for help with a talk I will soon give in Rimouski, at a gathering arranged by the Titanic Historical Society: what is important about the *Empress*?

"Well, we wouldn't have been born," Fred reflects. "Young Cyrus went to Calgary, Dad wanted to be with him after the war, he met Mom there, they went to California, and that's where we came in. All this happened because the *Empress* went down, and split up the family."

And disaster made for a closeness among the siblings, we agree. "Also it ties us to the people in Rimouski," Fred reasons. "People who were there for the survivors."

THE MOST
PERFECT RAINBOW

Many passengers and her crew
Went down with that old canoe
They all went down to never ride no more

This great ship was built by man
That is why she could not stand
She could not sink was the cry from one and all

But an iceberg ripped her side
And He cut down all her pride
They found the Hand of God was in it all

"Down with the Old Canoe"

EN ROUTE TO RIMOUSKI I stop over in Quebec City, where the *Queen Elizabeth II* has docked. Near its berth I fall into conversation with Louis Bolduc, the proprietor of a local antiquities shop. He admires the ending of the film *Titanic*.

"James Cameron, he was a genius-man," says Louis. "That scene on the grand staircase where they were clapping: what they meant was, 'Thanks for the chance to live again, in the movie!'"

Louis is interested in my story of forebears lost on the *Empress*. "May I tell you something?" says he. "My ancestor was an apothecary of Louis XIV, and he died in Versailles." Once, hearing Renaissance music performed there, Louis had a revelation: "My God, the others are all with us!" On this basis, he adds, *everybody* is with us *always*.

"Do you believe in the spirit of man?" Louis abruptly asks. For me this is an Are-you-saved kind of inquiry, and I respond with a few cold words about humanity's wish to annihilate itself.

Nonplussed, he assures me, "The spirit of your grandparents has not gone away." This is also doubtful, I suggest, in view of every generation's wish to leave the past behind.

Louis, a philosopher in an unphilosophic age, lends a few more *pensées*. Humanity is able to grasp the *intemporal* which is "beyond time and on the time — never finishing, *un mouvement perpetuel*," says he. "We are all primitives in front of the spirit of time — so we have to be small, to be a child."

Voyager of the Seas (distant left) and *Queen Elizabeth II*, Quebec City.
(David Creighton)

At sunrise the next morning, several Japanese are out with their tripods to shoot the QE2 moored below — the last of her kind, having been designed before jet travel took away the need for swift Atlantic voyages. She was built on the Clyde River, as was the *Empress;* and now its shipyards have trouble surviving.

The *Splendour of the Seas*, a Royal Caribbean cruise ship, comes into view and I go down to watch her come ashore. Here is the new breed of passenger liner, with numerous attractions on board and yet with none of yesteryear's sleek lines. For Louis such behemoths are not ships at all, but "floating hotels."

This one carries 1,800 passengers, to the QE2's 1,850 — a far cry from the Royal Caribbean's forthcoming *Voyager of the Seas*, with space for 3,100, being twice the size of the *Titanic*. She will have an 18-hole golf simulator, a four-storey shipping arcade, a 1,350-seat theatre replicating La Scala in Milan, a rock-climbing wall, an indoor ice rink with its own Zamboni.

A line from the *Splendour* bangs onto the pavement, handlers haul in the attached heavy rope to a bollard, those on deck pull in the slack. The process repeats itself until all is secure. I am able to visualize the *Empress*'s departure in reverse.

And just over at 110 rue St.-Pierre stands the old Bank of Montreal, to which the Purser's safe was brought for inspection after being raised by divers from the *Empress*. Claims against her were exorbitant (the same was true of the *Titanic*) and many packed the room to see an outpouring of riches.

The locksmith would briefly drill, study the results, and drill again — all morning long, until the safe's door yielded. Scarcely anything could be seen: cash and negotiable papers amounted to one-half percent of all that was claimed.

In London, the Lord Mayor set up a fund for *Empress* victims' families. But for the 353 widows and children it raised only 45,364 pounds, to which some 36,000 pounds gained in Canada were added — a far cry from the 430,780 pounds raised earlier for the *Titanic* fund.

"Been there, done that," Ballard remarked when I commented on this. World War I also deflected funds, generating many other priorities for public charity. And the *Storstad* yielded only $175,000 when sold at auction.

Arriving late at Notre Dame Basilica's sound-and-light show, *Act of Faith*, I am impressed: instead of verbal commentary, an otherworldly twitter accompanies the slides and phantasmagoric lights: brilliant! Then I notice earphones worn by those around me, and bend to tune into verbal commentary — which reduces it all to a mere lecture. When we might be experiencing mass in this ornate church.

And something is missing from our show, from this "historic multimedia adventure designed to come alive inside the unique Basilica of Notre-Dame de Québec an architectural masterpiece in its own right." Unmentioned, of course, is the Battle of the Basilica in 1887, pitting militant students against twenty-one marching Salvationists.

"As the blood ran down my neck and face," wrote Adjutant Robert McHardy in a letter to my grandfather, "my thought was carried back to when Jesus was all alone in the rough mob who were crying, 'Away with Him. Crucify him.' I then entered more fully into the reality of that heart-rending scene."

In Quebec, for decades no Army presence was allowed. So it was a thrill for me in 1998 to see officers of *l'Armée du Salut* beneath the Château Frontenac's chandeliers at our *dîner-bénéfice* — not drinking any wine, of course, but taking their rightful place in a more secularized Quebec.

Two blocks away at 14 Côte du Palais stands the Army's *Maison Ancrage*, Anchor House, *pour personnes avec différents problèmes de dépendance: alcoolisme, toxicomanie, dépendance affective, etc.* In the window, a Bible is open at the Beatitudes: "Blessed are the poor, for theirs is the kingdom of heaven."

Down at the Old Port of Quebec Interpretation Centre, mannequins portray immigrants on a ship's deck in the mid-nineteenth century: "Full of hope, they saw Quebec as their first contact with the New World." During the twentieth century's first decade, immigration reached an all-time peak as 2.6 million arrived in Canada.

And the Salvation Army, by 1914, had assisted over 150,000 to reach its shores. Yet by the time David became part of this plan, it was clear that slum dwellers, who lacked farm skills, would have required three costly weeks of preparation for the Canadian challenge; so the downtrodden of "darkest England" were excluded.

Even to bring over the "deserving" poor was an affront to organized labour here, angry that "agriculturists" would ultimately enter the industrial work force. Still, Ontario's premier praised the Army's service as "by far the best Immigration Agency which ever worked in this country."

In 1905 Rider Haggard, author of *King Solomon's Mines*, was sent by Britain's Colonial Secretary to report on Salvationist "Labour Colonies" in Canada. Much impressed, he saw heavy British immigration as an ideal way to relieve problems of injustice in the Empire — and also to forestall the Yellow Peril.

Haggard, pleasing the Colonial Secretary with his report, keenly inquired whether Prime Minister Arthur Balfour would be studying the fine print. "Oh, Arthur won't read it — you know, Arthur won't read it," the Secretary disclosed. The venture had been a pre-election ploy, meant to disarm two discerning critics at one go: Haggard himself, and William Booth.

In Rimouski the next morning, I ask a variety store clerk for *Empress* mementoes on sale. "This is about it," he replies, showing the liner portrayed on a phone card.

Well, what could I expect? The *Titanic's* legend brings heroic images easily to mind; for the *Empress*, there is no night to be remembered with any degree of uplift. At least for now.

En commémoration du **85** ième anniversaire du naufrage de l'*Empress of Ireland*

LaPuce 20 $

QuébecTel

www.quebectel.qc.ca/qtel/lapuce

QuebecTel phone card, 1999.

Strolling the town, I begin to feel mental vibrations. In the Tim Hortons I notice that four coffee pots are ready for use, and learn that in the wee hours a good number of yesterday's donuts are usually available; new batches are baked soon afterward. On May 29, 1914, Rimouski's backyard bread ovens would have been fired up early.

Opposite the cathedral, I find a commemorative marker giving the site of the Lepage general store; in 1914 its stock was emptied to provide for those made naked by disaster. *People who were there for the survivors.*

I stare into the windows of clothing shops downtown: Tendence, L'Elégance, Au Bon Goût d'Aujourd'hui, Friperie de l'Est, Centre de Liquidation. Summer clothing gives way to that of winter; in May of 1914, the process would have been reversed.

Many had lost everything — funds, personal items, attire — and townspeople clothed them in whatever way was possible. The railway station stands in its 1914 location; those arriving here to board the Quebec City train were a sight to behold, affliction having required gentlemen to go about in the overalls and heavy boots of what was then a farming community. There is a photograph of Salvationists in this unaccustomed garb.

Not yet is there a driving-tour pamphlet showing Empress sites around town, but a new hotel attracts visitors with a colourful ad declaring, "Welcome aboard! . . . You have a rendezvous with history! . . . greatest tragedy after the Titanic."

Hotel advertisement, Rimouski.

For me now, ordinary conveniences assume fresh meaning, as when I casually use a phone to call home. Only two or three lines led to the outer world in 1914, and these were heavily used by the press. Small wonder that not until the afternoon of the 29th did a clear message reach Toronto's Temple.

Two Salvationists undertook to transmit a first report of the disaster: Frank Morris, clad only in some chenille curtains, and Kenneth McIntyre, wearing a towel. All telegraph lines being tied up, they went to the telephone operator.

"We were curtly refused and asked where is the money coming from," said Morris. "They could see we were almost naked, but the money would have to be guaranteed."

At length Morris "pleaded and threatened" enough to contact the local manager, who even then denied service until Brigadier Rawling, in Montreal, was reached, and the sum of $5.50 immediately paid.

Bandsman Tom Greenaway, separated from his wife Mary when the boat sank, scoured the town seeking news of her. She had survived, yet without hope of seeing her husband again: "Tom's gone — I don't want to live." Mary was placed in a Rimouski hotel and here, seeing him enter, momentarily thought that he was a ghost before they embraced in tears.

A 1934 photo taken at the *Empress* memorial service shows the couple twenty years on, she in the dowdy attire worn by women during the Depression. Ted stands alongside David McAmmond, who told how Rees fought his way upstairs before going back down.

Next we see tall Ernest Green; Rufus Spooner, organizer of the "Dead Man" game; Alf Keith, who was warmed with a tablecloth on the *Storstad*. Further along stands Mary Attwell, who told of the large door opening to release the dead.

Here are Mr. and Mrs. Frank Brooks, unconnected with any *Empress* stories — for a reason evident from a *War Cry* reference: "Mrs. Brooks very ill at a hotel in Quebec": reporters were thus not on hand to interview them. Much quoted from the start, contrastingly, was Grace Hanagan — the pretty twenty-six-year-old married woman seen at the end.

Quite unknown is the site of the Rimouski schoolhouse used for a preliminary *Empress* inquest. It became the focus of world attention when Kendall, bruised and still in shock, lay back in an armchair to five evidence.

Empress survivors in 1934.
(George Scott Railton Heritage Centre)

The *Empress* had stopped because of the fog, he stated, and the *Storstad* ran into her. Later, not once would he stray from this assertion. But that gave cause for suspecting that he believed his ship was too close to the other: "We think," Lord Mersey later pronounced at Quebec City, "that he would have been better advised if he had given the *Storstad* a wider berth."

The old Rimouski Wharf is immediately west of a newer one comprising the marina. Survivors were delivered here, some almost beside themselves with terror and grief. Exposure killed twenty-two of them after rescue, claiming one woman's life here even as she was brought ashore.

The people of Rimouski, wheeling handcarts filled with clothing and food, met them here. All day they continued a grimmer responsibility: reclaiming the dead. These were laid out on the quayside and, when space ran out, in buildings requisitioned throughout the town.

Here I talk with Rodolphe, a local man fishing from the pier, about the Rimouski of old. A chill of astonishment hits me as I spot the QE2, sailing out to sea. "Look — there's the *Empress of Ireland!*" I burst out, eliciting laughter at this slip of the tongue. "No, no, I mean the *Queen Elizabeth II!*"

"It's not that either, because she hasn't been up the St. Lawrence for years," says Rodolphe. Then someone produces a pair of binoculars, and he agrees that the very ship is distantly passing by. If

Sudden storm at Rimouski, 1999.
(David Creighton)

215

I had been ten minutes earlier or later, chances are that nobody would have noticed.

The sky darkens as I begin walking back to the hotel, and a rainstorm swiftly descends — another whim of nature, like an errant iceberg or sudden fog patch. Racing for cover, I hear a car's horn and Rodolphe picks me up: Rimouski to the rescue once more.

Among the great *Empress* artifacts is a diary in a precise longhand for the year 1914, with brief marginal headings — "May 30 / Storm on Death Ship" — and neat underlinings that cast extra-important points into relief.

This is the diary of Gideon Miller. "Let's go out to see Gid," my father would say, and we would visit this gifted Salvationist officer at his Highland Creek home near Toronto. I remember his extensive reading — again, with notebook commentary on all books read — and his feeling for natural beauty.

Miller saw the Congress delegates off — *Gideon smiled most graciously at us from the wharf at Quebec,* David wrote — before taking the train back to Montreal. Here he visited the home of Brigadier John Rawlings, with whom he expected to spend a day.

At the front door was a Montreal *Star* special with large headlines. THE EMPRESS OF IRELAND / COLLISION S. S. STORSTAD IN THE GULF OF ST. LAWRENCE / ALL HANDS LOST. Rawlings had already left for his office, where he tried frantically for a through line to Rimouski. It took five hours.

Gideon later entrained with a colleague for Rimouski, to identify the bodies: "We secured an old lantern and in a shed at the end of the wharf on a heap of coal we counted 213 dead bodies. We found 16 Army comrades."

One paragraph, with "<u>A Lovely Smile</u>" in the margin, tells of a fisherman who said in broken English, "There's one I am sure belonging to you, she has lovely smile." This was Ernest Green's sister, Jessie, "and none looked more peaceful than she."

Gideon attended the schoolhouse inquest, giving this account:

> <u>Kendall called me over where he was seated and</u>
> <u>wanted to know how many people were lost. When</u>
> <u>I told him only 28 out of 171 [were saved], tears</u>
> <u>came to his eyes. He said he had planned this trip to</u>

be one of joy and gladness, with the chief officers of
the SA and the Staff Band and we were all keyed up
for a happy voyage, little thinking of sorrow, death
and disaster so near.

It was decided that Miller would accompany Salvationist remains
to Quebec City aboard a government steamer, the *Lady Grey*,
escorted by a cruiser of the North Atlantic squadron, the *Essex*. The
sky abruptly turned black with storm before clearing, to make one
side of the cruiser glisten with sunlight, the other remain dark with
cloud: "Just then the most perfect rainbow I ever saw formed an arch
over the mouth of the St .Lawrence reminding me of God's covenant
with man."

Next morning: "As we sailed near the shore I could hear the
birds singing and as we neared Quebec the church *bells rang out their
sweet music.*" Here is the sensitivity later to find expression in Miller's
design for the *Empress* memorial.

Then, arriving to face ten thousand people, with press
cameramen scaling telegraph poles for photo angles, Gideon
endured heavy strain once more:

People began rushing their dead to be embalmed. I was so afraid
they might get some of ours mixed with theirs. I stayed around that
room till 6 p.m. when we placed the last coffin in a CPR car for
Toronto and just then who should I meet but Mr. Miles and Stone
undertakers from Toronto wanting to know if they could help in any
way. I told them we had just placed the last coffin in the car and I
was hungry and dirty. They invited me to dinner with them in one of
the large hotels.

FROM THE NEW WORLD

The Titanic generates interest because it generates interest. It is an icon because it is an icon. In this way a good story can prolong itself indefinitely.

Steven Biel, *Down with the Old Canoe*

CHECKING INTO THE HOTEL Rimouski to join Titanic Historical Society members, I find among them a *Titanic* survivor, Millvina Dean. Among the very last now, she is a sprightly 87. Having been only seven weeks old at the time of disaster, she holds no recollection of rescue in her mother's arms on the fateful night.

Titanic survivor Millvina Dean.
(David Creighton)

Off we go to the Musée de la Mer, where David Saint.-Pierre gives background: "The *Empress* dropped her pilot right here, a half-hour before she sank." Several respond to this with an *Ohhhh* of wonderment; a very keen audience.

I am pleased to meet THS's low-key founder, Ed Kamuda. He tells about William Tantum, whose wish to find the *Titanic* was born here on the St. Lawrence where the *Empress* sank. Ed recalls Tantum's wish for republication of important books about both of these shipwrecks; "He was like a booster rocket to us, a second founder."

We next visit the Institut Maritime du Québec's downtown campus, first to see demonstrations by the staff — early diving technique, engine room procedure, navigation, radar simulation — and then for yet another *Titanic* dinner: Canapes a l'amiral, Consomme Olga, Saumon poche sauce mousseline, Filet mignon Lili, Salade d'asperges avec champagne, Eclairs au chocolat, Assortiment de fruit frais et fromage, Cigares et porto.

The menu is printed on a computer-modified still from *Titanic*, showing Digital Domain's 1/20th-scale model with computer-generated people aboard. "Imagine we're making a commercial for White Star Lines," James Cameron instructed, "and we need beautiful shots sweeping around the ship from a helicopter." Much as in Partisan's *Empress* shoot on the *Night Wind*.

Sitting opposite me is Doug Secord, heroic Dr. James Grant's look-alike grandson, who gives a brief talk. He quotes from Grant's own account of disaster: "Several hundred clung to the ship . . . screaming for help, shrieking . . . caught like rats in a trap."

Afterwards we talk about the manic-depression suffered by Grant in later years. Was this connected with his 1914 experience? One of Grant's sons took his own life, Doug remarks. The anguish caused by sudden loss, the likelihood of enduring trauma — I mention a parallel with Edith Creighton's malady. No doubt the causes are similar, we agree.

Childhood memories of Ernest Green are given by his grandson, Major David Ivany: "I see him as a seventy-five-year-old man, standing on a wharf in Muskoka — stretching, kicking his legs, then diving off to swim with strong strokes."

At the time, little did David realize, that on the night of May 29 Green survived in the St. Lawrence's cold water because of his

R.M.S. Titanic
14 avril 1912

Canapés à l'amiral

Consommé Olga

Saumon poché sauce mousseline

Filet mignon Lili

Salade d'asperges avec champagne

Éclairs au chocolat

Assortiment de fruit frais et fromages

Cigares et porto

Titanic-style
dinner menu,
Rimouski, 1999.

swimming ability, and through the good fortune of finding that life-jacketed corpse.

Green lost his sister and both parents, but would always speak of hope. "The torch was passed to me," says David, concluding that we all travel on an imperilled boat, metaphorically, and owe each other the care that will bring us through. He quotes from an Army hymn: "Whatever the future, His ways are best you see."

An accordionist plays, dedicating one number to Millvina Dean: "I composed this on the St. Lawrence, one very cold night." He switches to a waltz, and a Rimouski couple at my table gets up to dance. Hearty Salvationism, and Quebecois joie-de-vivre: both come together now.

In my talk I explain that Bertha and David Creighton left five orphans, that my father shortly went to war, that he hauled ammunition to kill the enemy and collected the dead. No sentiment from me tonight.

Repeating Louis Bolduc's question, whether I believe in the spirit of man, I tell how hard it is to hold such a faith today.

Christian humanism, as shown by the Salvation Army's concern for even the ungodliest creatures: fine. Its values strengthened my forebears at a time of grief, and two relatives' families gave the youngest orphans all the love that anyone could ask for. I believe in that kind of devotion and caring.

Then there's the spirit-of-man ideology of a fascist New Order or a communist paradise or an American Way. Come on, Louis, in our century over 160 million lives have been taken by those serving such dubious causes — and by the imperialism that once gave ocean liners the name *Empress*.

I tell about standing where my father had stood in Tournai, and searching for what he had felt near the beginning of what some call the Seventy-Five Years War. The human evil he saw was bound to repeat itself, on a far more demonic scale. And we can only keep our fingers crossed that war won't resume its escalation.

What to believe? I put stock in what Jesus says about those inheriting the Kingdom — "I was hungry and you fed me, I was thirsty and you gave me drink, I was a stranger and you took me in, I was naked and you clothed me."

I tell how on May 29, 1914, the townspeople would have knocked on one another's doors: *"Un grand désastre! . . . Aidez! . . . Assistez!"* Down to Rimouski Wharf they came, with food and attire and consolation.

Mentioning the *Empress* shoot aboard the *Night Wind*, I speak about emotional need. How Rimouski people again bought comfort. How Real the helmsman put a hand on my shoulder when he said, "Anyway, enjoy the sunshine — while we're still alive." At such moments, I conclude, one may well believe in the spirit of man.

Next morning a bus takes us to Ste.-Luce-sur-Mer Church, for a memorial service to be conducted jointly by its Catholic priest and Salvation Army officers. "Safety in numbers," someone remarks, noting how churchgoing has declined in recent years.

First off, I see that the choir occupies a loft above the west door, just like in Tournai. And again there is great music. To hear young voices rendering "Nearer My God to Thee," here in this beautiful church, is to sense the hymn's true power — emphasizing not so much a departure from life as a fervent approach to the divine.

Emotions rise a notch higher as the Reverend Guy Lagace enters side by side with a uniformed Salvationist, David Ivany. The idea of such reconciliation is one thing, the reality quite another: magnificent.

"The movie *Titanic* shows a relation between two classes, how love will transcend differences," Ivany states. "When disaster occurred here in 1914, the people of Rimouski shared clothing with *Empress of Ireland* survivors, not caring about social rank and only concerned with helping. And we're here today, united."

Ivany picks up his cornet, asks that we now think of God's grace, and plays "Amazing Grace" with organ accompaniment. Then comes the Biblical text, from *Romans*: "Who shall separate us from the love of Christ? shall tribulation, or distress, or persecution, or famine, or nakedness, or peril, or sword? As it is written, For thy sake we are killed all day long."

David tells how at the *Empress*'s departure, staff band members played "O Canada," and "Old Lang Syne." Then, "God Be with You Till We Meet Again": the sacred song "floated over the water." And now we hear David's wife, Beverly, sing that very hymn.

On the morning of April 29, 1914, the Peterborough Temple Band arrived in Montreal, intending to board the *Alaunia* for passage to the Congress. Immediately its members were shocked to learn the *Empress*'s fate, and briefly thought of returning home. Then in Montreal's streets the band played "Nearer My God to Thee" and "God Be with You Till We Meet Again": songs of the *Titanic* and *Empress* brought together.

Our service makes the same juxtaposition: one hymn that could well have been played at a ship's demise, the other at the start of a supposedly happy voyage.

Those Peterborough musicians resolved to continue down the St. Lawrence, and at 2 a.m. when the *Alaunia* passed the sunken liner, they gathered at the deck rail as the bandmaster threw a memorial wreath. All marvelled, it was said, at "the mysterious circumstances that brought about such a grievous loss." Then, further down the river at dawn, they beheld material evidence of disaster: an *Empress* lifeboat, floating toward the sea.

Empress lifeboat, photographed from *Alaunia* on May 30, 1914.
(George Scott Railton Heritage Centre)

As the service ends, yet another emotional haymaker is delivered. Beverly, now at the organ, plays the slow movement of Antonin Dvorak's Ninth Symphony, the choir singing along.

As in Tournai, I climb to the choir loft for a closer approach to this music. Beverly sits in her Army uniform at the organ, choir members gathered around to sing the words.

Beverly Ivany playing
Dvorak.
(David Creighton)

Again and again Beverly plays the theme, drawing out emotion the way Salvationists do with song-book choruses during holiness meetings. The singers can't get enough of this tune, nor can I.

Someone arranged this Czech melody as a Negro spiritual with the words "Goin' Home" — wrongheaded, in a sense, but also right inasmuch as Dvorak used it in an opera to suggest a man's longing for his family, home, and garden.

This is called the New World Symphony, and thus has a special resonance in terms of my grandfather's toil of bringing thousands to Canada, before death came on the very pathway of immigration.

Second movement, *Largo*, Antonin Dvorak's Symphony No. 9: "From the New World." The last note is played, and in the fullness of my heart I give Beverly a prolonged embrace. Releasing herself finally she utters, perhaps more in good humour than alarm, a fervent *amen*.

IN THE CABIN
FOR THE NIGHT

*As Jack and Rose embrace at the bow rail, they DISSOLVE
SLOWLY AWAY, leaving the ruined bow of the WRECK ...*
James Cameron,
Screenplay for *Titanic*

L OVE AND DEATH: THE *Titanic* story has both, in spades. "We have
been living together for many years, and where you go I go,"
said Ida Straus to husband Isador, according to steward Alfred
Crawford at the Senate Investigation. Cameron's *Titanic* shows the
aged couple in bed together, rotating in the water as it rises.

Could my grandparents have experienced such a *Liebestod*? Bertha
was only 42 and David was 50. On that night she was finally there in
the cabin with her husband — who had just written his spirited note
to the Festive Board — at the start of her very first ocean-liner
voyage. Circumstances for intimacy.

Still alive today is our sole link with the generation that knew
the tragedy first-hand — Violet, Wilfred's second wife. She has a
story about Bertha and David.

Having survived a major fight with cancer, my aunt is now 98.
Visiting Vi at the Guelph home of her daughter Win, I hear again
a familiar series of anecdotes. First, the one about Wilfred's Model
T Ford, in which she took special pride and, once, gave it a
uniquely shiny black surface: "Nugget shoe polish — I did the
whole car."

Vi is English-born, from Parkstone near Bournemouth. Of her
ten siblings, one was a miner named George who, weary of the pits
one day, "came home, showed his family a map of Canada, said
goodbye and was gone." Later, he pitched in to buy a fare to Canada
for Vi and her sister Pearl.

Wilfred's first marriage was to Dora Jacobs, whose sister was the
wife of *Empress* survivor Ernest Green. Dora contracted tuberculosis
and perished while giving birth at the Ontario Hospital in
Gravenhurst. Then the baby, brought by him to another hospital in
Toronto, died as well.

Wilfred Creighton
with first wife
Dora Jacobs.

Wilfred became a nervous wreck, unable for two years to speak to another girl. Then one night after songster practice at the Yorkville Corps, he said to Vi, "Wait for me, I'm going your way." Vi decided not to wait, taking the streetcar — but he managed to catch up to her in his Model T, on Danforth at Broadview, and beeped his horn.

"One toot and I got out," she tells me now, some eighty years on. "That was the start of our marriage." Their honeymoon was at the farm acquired recently by Edith and her husband.

Mischievously I ask how the newlyweds spent their two weeks in this rural setting. "You could go down the hill and there was a river," says Vi, recalling what we knew as the Creek. "We'd go down by the river, I guess."

From the Bolton farm our memories progress to the modest one where Vi herself was a shepherdess, on the Pacific Mall's site. A 1966 photo shows my aunt feeding one of her lambs from a bottle. Maternal devotion otherwise directed to her descendants — she now has a dozen great-grandchildren — was readily given to these creatures as well. "Perhaps that's why the Lord let me live so long," she allows.

Mentally we roam a forgotten world of Chinese laundries, radios made by hand, Sussex ("quite a Creighton place"), bread fried in bacon grease, orders taken for eggs, a store that sold hand-picked wild raspberries. "It was quite interesting," says Vi.

As usual I bring conversation around to the *Empress*, to hear once more Violet's story about my grandparents' fate. "He tried to save her," she says. How that can be known is hard to imagine, their bodies never having been found. Yet perhaps she heard of such a struggle from Wilfred — who just possibly might have learned of this from survivors in a tale otherwise unrecorded.

"They were in the cabin for the night," she states. This, we may assume, is true.

Violet Creighton, the last of her generation.

"It's quite interesting when you think back," says Vi as memory turns toward the old East Toronto corps. "Sunday's our busy day. Wilf goes off for the band."

A 1946 photo shows the citadel's prominent biblical text, mounted behind the platform. Here are Will and Wilfred with their sons — Fred, Gord, Arthur — united in service to the Kingdom.

In the middle stands Gord, the second son, who died of leukemia. The most humorous of my cousins, he once recounted how he and his bride went to Montreal in a car with a trailer behind and it took them almost three days to go those four hundred miles; after a brief drive, they would get the urge to stop and enter the trailer. He told this to me and my father — who never advised me about sex — and I was amazed to see that Will found this as funny as I did.

Creighton bandsmen at East Toronto corps, 1946.

Art Creighton, Vi's third child and the only descendant to serve lifelong as an officer, entered Salvationist work on hearing a radio documentary about the *Empress of Ireland*. "I realized that my grandfather was actually on that ship," he said. "And after I went to sleep, the Lord called me to give myself for officership and take Grandpa's place."

His sister Win also became an officer and married one, Howard Crossland, to serve in small corps on the prairies. Occasionally at Sunday meetings no worshippers would show up; and to avoid giving satisfaction to United Church rivals across the street, Win would loudly play the organ as if things had gone swimmingly.

Evangelism concluded when Howard brought the family to Florida, where he became a plumber at Walt Disney World.

"It's interesting when you look back," Vi again remarks. Time for her is a span of human memory all the way back to Jesus and the Old Testament kings.

She consults her watch, which compensates for her near-blindness by speaking the time aloud. "I call her Flo," she remarks. "She lies — when it's 1:30 she says 1:50."

Time to go. Before I leave, Win gives me a ledger book with

cash-and-balance notations by our grandfather. The well bound little
volume begins on January 1, 1901 and runs into 1910, late-March
notations being squeezed onto the inside back cover:

31/3/10 Wilfred (allowance) 2.10
    "   Willie (")   2.00
    "   Edith   (")   2.15

Apportionments are not quite by age, the largest going to Edith
— probably for her responsibilities toward Arthur and Cyrus.

There would have been another such booklet, taking the
account into mid-May of 1914. I know this because of a sentence in
the last letter David wrote to his children: "Enclosed is the note &
will which you will have placed in that little ledger book."

Salvationists view souls in terms of a strict account held by God.
Each human life, no matter how lowly, is the focal point of a
dramatic conflict between good and evil. It is a struggle destined to
bring about the Kingdom of God.

Karen Armstrong, a former Roman Catholic nun, describes this
in *The Battle for God*. Two paths to the truth, *logos* and *mythos*, were
once seen as alternatives. "*Logos* was the rational, pragmatic, and
scientific thought that enabled men and women to function well in
the world," she states. "The *mythos* of a society provided people with
a context that made sense of their day-to-day lives; it directed their
attention to the eternal and the universal."

Once, both were felt to be essential. Now that *logos* becomes the
basis of society, *mythos* is widely viewed as something from the past.
The Christian narrative of redemption becomes only one element in
comparative mythology, a rational discipline.

So Robert Ballard, suffering bereavement, turns to Joseph
Campbell for solace. Organized religion is thus diminished.. Yet on the
Night Wind that afternoon, hovering between today's consciousness and
that of ancestors whose remains lay below, I saw its merits as never
before. Think of what those Salvationists at the East Toronto corps
gleaned from worship: fellowship, ritual, transcendence, a channel for
love, focus, a context that "made sense of their day-to-day lives."

THE HEAD AND THE HEART

Je me souviens.
I remember.

Motto of the Province of Quebec

WITHOUT THE ABILITY TO forget there is too much pain;
but a life without memories is devoid of context,
richness, depth.

For more *Empress* remembrances, I head down to the opening of
Rimouski's 3-D museum restaging her doom. En route, I stop off at
Montreal to witness a moment of immediate history: *Canadiens* star
Maurice "Rocket" Richard's state funeral, abounding with parallels to
Empress memorial rites back in 1914.

Empress funeral, Mount Pleasant Cemetery.
(George Scott Railton Heritage Centre)

Again, a hockey rink is used for the lying-in-state. In the Molson Centre, past Richard's open casket file 600,000 mourners: "captains of industry and common folk, young and old, in business suits and sundresses" — a scene resembling that observed by Gideon Miller: *The Arena was crowded with people of all creeds and classes, with thousands outside.*

Articles describe Richard, the most electrifying scorer in hockey's annals, as a working-class hero. A "straight arrow," married to the same woman for fifty-one years. A gentle family man. Someone "never motivated by money," who hurled himself into action for the pure love of his calling, "driven only by courage and instinct."

These are Salvationist values, and Torontonians showing respect to the *Empress* dead in 1914 would have honoured those values. The fearless Rocket once was suspended from Stanley Cup play for all-out attack on a rival player, and angry Montrealers responded with the infamous Richard Riots. Yet he came to be "all things to all people" — as did the Salvation Army, after being persecuted for the fiery boldness by which it brought religion to the working class.

At the Molson Centre as its garage doors open and the hearse is driven forth, Richard's most ardent fans chant *Mau-reece! Mau-reece!* I follow the cortège down the rue Ste-Catharine, where rioters surged forty-five years ago. No music, no massed bands as at this very time of year in 1914 — but a solid wave of applause pulses all along the route.

Maurice Richard funeral procession, May 31, 2000.
(David Creighton)

Before Notre Dame the coffin is lifted from the hearse, and solemnly borne inside as a clangour of churchbells breaks out. On a giant TV screen we then observe the unfolding of old-fashioned rites for the soul of Maurice Richard. These attain an emotional climax at 11:50 as Ginette Reno, a favourite *chanteuse* of Richard's, sings *Ceux Qui S'en Vent*. "Those Who Go Away": a pop-Qébecois parallel to *God Be With You Till We Meet Again*.

On square Dominion I revisit a figure of John A Macdonald, Confederation's point man, held within a shrine resembling the Albert Memorial. It has a new head, vandals having cut off the old one in 1992 on November 16 — the well-remembered day on which Louis Riel was hanged for treason. Indian-French hunters and farmers in Manitoba, overwhelmed by the tide of white immigration and denied title to their farms, rose under Riel in the failed North-West Rebellion.

Men soon to help in putting down the insurrection were in Saint John, as we have seen, at the very moment when my grandfather was joining a spiritual army. Riel's execution secured the West for white-European settlement: this was the price paid for David's humanitarian work of abetting immigration.

Further north on rue Clark, my grandparents lived during David's social-work stint here in 1902-6. Bertha formed lasting bonds with French soldiers at the local corps. A postcard later sent to her by a Madame Cabril offered a Versailles vista and this bilingual message:

> *Dear Good Friend:*
>
> *How are you? Despite my silence, I don't forget you. Tonight I leave dear France, it's hard to do. Say hello to dear Major and and the children. See you soon.*
>
> There is no place like home.

The Clark Street home was later demolished to provide a back entrance to the former Baron Byng High School, fictionalized by ex-student Mordecai Richler in *Adventures of Duddy Kravitz*.

At "Fletcher's Field High," Duddy goes through the same cadet-march capers I knew at Malvern Collegiate in Toronto (Glenn Gould tramping the streets with all the rest of us). It surprised me that

Hollywood bestowed attention on our rites of Empire, Richard Dreyfuss donning Canadian khaki as Duddy in the film version. Still inside the school are aged trophy cases — ours during World War II showed photos of fallen alumni — which now display laurels won by a Sun Youth Organization.

Ravenscrag, named after a medieval Scottish castle, looms above on Mount Royal. Shipowner Hugh Allan was often seen with telescope each week at its tower's upper windows, awaiting the arrival of his steamer from Glasgow. He was also a banker and the back-room boss of many firms, given near-monopolistic power by government subsidies. Allan's steamship company, absorbed later by Canadian Pacific, became the kernel of its Atlantic Service employing *Empress* liners.

McGill University spreads out below. Here, economics professor Stephen Leacock year by year "saved the British Empire" in his Arts Building lectures. The *University Magazine*, edited by his close friend Andrew Macphail, painted the Empire as a noble alternative to any link with America and its extremes of wealth. Canadians were viewed as stawarts rooted in the British soil.

This was essentially the Creightons' view of the country — and much of our humour, you might say, was in Leacock's vein. On the *Empress's* last voyage at least one passenger is known to have been reading his *Sunshine Sketches of a Little Town*, which includes a very widely known Canadian shipwreck tale: the comic sinking of the *Mariposa Belle.* This Harland and Wolff steamer goes down, Leacock emphatically points out, at the very moment that voices rise in singing "O Canada."

You may rest assured about "the solidity of the British connection" when sailing on the *Mariposa Belle* with Orangemen about, waving their flags. But dread strikes the passengers on this voyage as water suddenly pours in "at every seam." Then Mr Smith of Smith's Hotel, after collecting bets about the vessel's fate, guilefully gets her floating by deftly plugging those seams and "brings her in," all the richer.

It may be surmised that this shyster, conveying anthem-singing Canadians to safety, represents money-making America. If so, it would be is prophetic: during World War I as Canada sought funds to keep her military effort afloat, its Conservative government was advised by financially-strapped Britain to go to Wall Street. Which it did: a decisive turning-point of empires.

Contributing verse to the *University Magazine* in that era was a doctor named John McCrae, who later penned lines set down in the Canadiens' dressing-room wall at the Forum: that old message about a torch to be passed and held high.

The team's new home adjoins the former Windsor Station, with its statue of George Stephen: "First President / the Canadian Pacific Railway/1881-1888." Fourteen tracks used to originate here. How many tens of thousands set off from this spot for the West and for war service? The CPR war memorial presents a angel-cradling-slain-warrior motif echoing that of a *Grand Guerre* statue before Sartre's high school in Le Havre.

At Richard's funeral we bade farewell to an imperial era when unassuming dignity was a way of life. He became the ultimate role model for people taught to be compassionate in peaceful times, and killers during combat.

Continuing to Quebec City and the Museum of Civilization to see its permanent show, *Mémoires*, I find in semi-darkness a statue of Queen Victoria with her head blown off. The 1963 explosion that did this, awaking all of Quebec City, figures in Leonard Cohen's novel *Beautiful Losers* — the dynamite charge being placed "in her metal lap."

All across the Empire, as it collapsed during the 1960s, Victoria's statues disappeared from public view. No other human being had been so memorialized. Here, violation of the royal image signalled Quebec's Quiet Revolution.

A generation later, with *globalization* an inescapable buzzword, Britain's empire excites new interest. Now I read that superstar Jean Beliveau, describing a final visit to the ailing Richard, gives the date as May 22, "the Queen's birthday." A Quebecker's respectful word bestowed on this imperial emblem, this ruler over Anglo domains!

The Richard Riots are often cited as a precursor of Sixties unrest. A comment made about the Rocket by Maple Leaf coach Pat Quinn (of obvious Irish descent) puts this initiative into broader Canadian terms: "He symbolized the desire to get out from under the British flag, that we were no longer a colony and had to stand on our own as a country."

Imperialism was cast off by Anglos and Quebeckers both, the latter also giving up, a bred-in-the-bone Christian resignation. *La résignation Chrétienne*, doing one's appointed earthly task without deviance or complaint, this went on for centuries until a nationalist urge finally surfaced. Old values then gave way to newer ones exalting entrepreneurial drive and the industrial state.

It is hard now to imagine a nationalism once embracing all of Canada within an imperial context. Carl Berger tried to perceive that ideal from within, writing a book called *The Sense of Power*. Canadians could "assert their authority over the Empire," it was felt, through conferences made possible by advanced communication modes. And Canadian nationality was seen as extending over time as well as space, in a comprehension of the past; thus it "rested upon a certain understanding of history, the national character, and the national mission."

In Rimouski, from the bus depot I walk to the *Musée de la Mer* on a route paralleling the St. Lawrence. This leads past the CPR memorial, where Robert Ballard was filmed from all angles during our shoot. Rightly so, this riverside *Empress* monument being in a notably solemn location. And underneath are the dead, many unidentified.

A house newly built on the riverside now partially obscures the view. Unnecessary, upsetting. And the annual Memorial Day service at Mount Pleasant Cemetery, I am told, has been discontinued "for lack of interest."

Robert Ballard at CPR *Empress* monument.
(David Creighton)

So to memorialize the disaster, much now depends on perspectives the media will provide.

Soon visible at Father Point is a pair of new buildings, one tilted as if by a gust of wind and another of normal foundation. Each sprouts a slanted mesh cylinder representing — the *Empress's* funnels. A connecting hall is now occupied by visitors assembled for the opening.

At once I ask Shanti, a guide, about that special effect meant to portray the *Storstad's* prow piercing a stateroom. "Yes, it will be shown going into the *Empress* but just by a *symbole*," she affirms. "The floor is red that's the *Empress*, the yellow is the *Storstad*, you see this clearly from the top of the lighthouse." When I have trouble grasping this, she laughs: "We will put some rock there to show how big was the *Storstad!*"

So far so good: I never wanted that image to be graphically realized. Then the museum's tilted half, opened to inspection, turns out to have a level floor and numerous low-tech accounts of *Empress* liners: a lot of things to read. There is also someone's colour movie of a crossing — which underlines for me, having done that Atlantic route once on the Italian Line, how boring such trips could be.

I receive my ticket for a first showing of the new *Empress* movie, presented in the other building. Glasses lending a 3-D effect are given out. We enter a small theatre where shipwreck debris is visible at the sides behind translucent screens. The movie begins.

Première représentation

Ticket for showing of Empress movie at Musée de la Mer.

Here is Commissioner Rees, as if in the round, at the railing once more. Now attention shifts to a young girl, "Anna," sailing the *Empress* with her family on what is hoped to be a visit to their Polish homeland. "Sandboxes, they're for babies!" Anna complains to her mother — alluding to an *Empress* play area — then wilfilly sets forth on a tour of the boat.

By 3-D magic, old photos of the ship's interior form a sepia background for our Anna, shown in shimmering white. "The steward wanted to close our portholes," she remarks, "but my mother wouldn't let him come into the cabin." A key explanatory note, deftly delivered.

"Object starboard side!" the watch abruptly shouts. Engines are put into "full reverse" to no avail, and water is seen rushing through one of those portholes so negligently left open.

"Take my life vest, I'll find another," orders Sir Henry Seton-Karr in the grand imperial tradition of *being British*. Choral music plays as actors face destiny on what seems to be the upturned hull. A floating doll represents the 134 children who, like Anna, perished by shipwreck.

Finally, names of the dead roll in alphabetical order: First Class, then Second Class — but only down to the Bs, just before my grandparents would have been mentioned. A jarring omission.

"Too much *Titanic*," says David Staint Pierre, referring to a shot of one funnel toppling from its base — as never occurred on the *Empress* — and other motifs borrowed from James Cameron's film.

What about those initial plans for the show as promised at the Benefit Banquet: *robots appearing, elements of the scenery moving, artificial fog?* "That was the *first* concept," David answers. "The audience would end up on the floor!"

The film is haunting nonetheless in its use of an old Polish tale, about a dragon with fiery breath. Anna has a bad dream of entering this monster, and trying to escape. Water pours onto its flame and the dragon "roars and hisses" — metaphorically, the boilers are flooded — in an evocation of poetic legend, to which the Québecois soul forever responds.

Interesting that the film should centre on someone who in 1914 would have been called a "foreigner." The *Globe*, describing Hamilton's *Empress* death toll, listed twenty *Empress* passengers with obviously Anglo-Saxon names, and then added that "a number of foreigners" were also aboard.

The Times of Hamilton also provided no names of ethnic victims, while graphically recording their relatives' plight: "Everybody seemed to be calling on everybody else, and it was late in the day when the real state of affairs was impressed upon them, since they were unable to grasp the fact of the disaster."

Even Salvationists used that term "foreigner" from the pre-multicultural past. The *Star* quotes Alfred Keith as saying, "Our boat picked up a foreigner who had gone crazy with the shock and tried to get out." Rufus Spooner, similarly, tells of seeing an officer "punch a big foreigner who tried to rush past and into the boat out of his turn."

Imperialism has fled, and with it a mindset that assigned lesser rights to women, to the working class, to those of undesirable speech and bearing. To correct much of this injustice during a mere half-century since the loss of empire — by Britain and by a dozen other world powers — is a moral achievement of considerable scope.

I have booked a berth on the VIA passenger train back to Montreal, scheduled to leave Rimouski at 12:28 a.m. To stay awake until then I contrive a trail of donut shops and pizza places and retro eateries, remaining conscious as I sample the fare at each for a half-hour or so, before moving on.

Of course, my grandparents lost consciousness forever on that night eighty-six years ago. And on entering my train at last, I take the journey they never had — only a few Salvationists having thus left the disaster site. This gives so much to think about that I can't get to sleep until we're beyond Rivière-du-Loup.

I have my continental breakfast in a dome car from the 1950s, with other railroaders taking an early-morning look at our land. Here, away from the highway and its fast-food outlets, is a chaste landscape — field and forest, river and stream — much as my grandparents might have seen it. Halting briefly in Drummondville, our long silver-and-blue train takes up all the middle of town.

"This man won't bite you," says Gloria to her grandson who, placed beside me, becomes absorbed in the angles of our adjustable foot rests.

"Press that and it goes down, I *noticed* it," four-year-old Nicholas informs me. "You have to pull up the GO pedal, that's the gas it makes it stop it's *foh real*." An elderly rail buff, drawn from his revery by this clatter of metal and speech, chastises him. In Nicholas I see

Officer's record for David Creighton.

young Cyrus, also 4 back in 1914, whose parents departed from his life upon being promoted to glory.

Every June I travel by bus down the eastern seaboard and on to Mexico City, then up the west coast and over into Quebec to complete the circle. Sixteen cities in three weeks: I love the convoluted history of these places, the contrasting moods, the people. On the first Saturday — which is now — I always hit Lowell, Massachusetts.

This is the home town of Jack Kerouac, another Greyhound wanderer, famous for being *on the road*. He was of Québecois descent and, like Maurice Richard, a star athlete who identified himself with ordinary people while holding true to Catholicism. Richard's kinfolk were from east of Rimouski (rural Gaspé) and Kerouac's from just to the west (Riviere-du-Loup and nearby St. Pacôme). The latter's birthdate was 1922, one year after Richard's and eight before my own.

If I ever understand the real Kerouac, I'll know myself as well: split between Christianity and hedonism, highway and home, American and Canadian outlooks, this world and something transcending it. Also, he was of a family deeply affected by bereavement.

Afternoon wanes as I reach Lowell and walk over into Little Canada, once inhabited by immigrant Quebeckers. Across the Merrimack River I find many homes displaying plaster images of Mary.

Denominational icons, before branding went secular. Religion pervading daily life. My childhood world of belief in the divine, in salvation, in a world beyond our own.

Backyard shrine in Lowell, Massachusetts.

At 34 Beaulieu in 1926 Gerard Kerouac, the writer's nine-year-old brother, died from *purpura hemorragica*: bleeding with such force that he suffocated, writhing in pain.

The border between this life and the beyond: Kerouac, then only 3, experienced the contrast in a way that governed the rest of his life. That is what interests me about this address, one block from the Catholic elementary school where Gerard's visions of the afterlife had astonished the nuns.

When death unmercifully claims a child — young Cyrus also in 1926, David's brother Herbert in 1881, "Anna" and those 134 young *Empress* victims — what then? In *Visions of Gerard*, Kerouac reconstructs the immensity of Gabrielle Kerouac's grief.

My mother's upstairs sobbing, lost all her control now.

". . . They took him off to Heaven! — They didnt leave him with me! — Gerard, my little Gerard!"

"Calm yourself, poor Ange, you've suffered so."

"I havent suffered like he did, that's what *breaks* my heart!" and she yells that and they all know she really means it, she's had her fill of the injustice of it, a little lame boy dying without hope — "it's *that* that's tearing my heart out and breaking my head in two!"

"Ange, Ange, poor sensitive heart!" weeps gentle Aunt Marie at her shoulder.

Nin and I are sobbing horribly in bed side by side to hear these pitiful wracks of clack talk coming from our own human mother, the softness of her arms all gashed now in the steely proposition Death-

"I'll never be able to wipe that from my memory!" — "Not as long as I live!" — "He died *without* a chance!"

"We all die -"

"Good, damn it, good!" she cries, and this sends chills thru all of us man and child and the house is One Woe this night.

Somewhat different was the Creightons' situation in 1914: a mourning for parents, not for a sickly child. Yet during those long hours of affliction at 136 Hogarth, could Edith or Will or anyone else have collapsed in a way such as Kerouac describes?

The orphans' response to their parents' hideous demise will remain a mystery. Of the days when four-year-old Cyrus and the others began to grasp the horror, little may now be gleaned except what the *War Cry* and *Young Soldier* report. *Conditions prevailing beggar description. Sorrow and grief prevail everywhere.*

Was there no outrage? No questioning, no disbelief in the hope of salvation? Did the head, counselling despair, not veto the heart that longs for faith?

Edith would never be the same, and Will would later disconnect from Salvationism;but Wilfred held firm.

LOST LINERS

WHEN *Lost Liners* IS telecast on July 12, my relatives marvel at all the air time bestowed on the *Empress*. The consensus is that it represents our clan well without being too florid.

For some, it means little but pain. "I couldn't talk after the program, just thinking about what happened," says Barbara, Arthur's daughter. "I always resented them for leaving the five children." She has a dread of being left behind: his plight recurring in her own life.

"Daddy did very well for an orphan boy," Barbara remarks. But sometimes, Arthur would not speak for lengthy periods — until one of his brothers showed up and his usual self would reappear; "then he'd go back into silence."

Robert, her brother, takes a different view of the family's situation following disaster: "One, the ages were spread out; two, our grandfather made specific plans. And Wilfred always had an aim in his mind, of reuniting everybody."

Lost Liners puts focus on the Canadian Pacific, Arthur's employer, and on the immigration trade in which he played a role. Here is a glimpse beyond the familiar National Dream epic into its ocean-spanning sequel with a tragic turn of events.

Yet the documentary receives scant notice in the local press, and this is a story in itself. One program guide describes for July 12 a British "reality TV" series and a Christmas/Hanukah tale, ignoring *Lost Liners*. Another highlights our show but omits reference to the *Empress*. A third mentions the boat while providing an illustration of the *Lusitania's* nameplate. Only one connects the program to our land — albeit erroneously, stating that the *Empress* "sank off the Canadian coast."

None of the listings-compilers, apparently, could identify what Ballard describes as "Canada's greatest maritime disaster." Here was a two-hour special providing lavish detail, yet some of my friends picked it up only through random channel-surfing. For similar documentaries Peter Schnall has won a half-dozen Emmies — by incurring costs of $500,000 an hour (as opposed to $200,000 for the average History Channel show), by avoiding stock footage, by shooting in film rather than videotape.

So if this effort fails to catch the Canadian eye, it is hard to imagine what will. Losing the *Empress* all over again — or so it would seem.

And James Cameron's *Titanic*, telling a shipwreck story that never happened, becomes a megahit. Some Creightons refuse to see it. But who can fault this *genius-man* for tackling the great legend of failed technology, and for declaring a kind of hope? When Rose swims over to blow that officer's whistle, I am as thrilled as anyone else by her will to live.

Sentiment, of course.

My cousin Barbara, knowing what the *Empress* disaster did to Arthur, sees only the torment. Reliving it through the documentary, she visualized Jesus dying on the cross by divine plan. "I can't see that as a compassionate God," she reflects. "Life is a pretty cruel joke, isn't it?"

Yet Robert, often face to face with suffering at Sick Children's Hospital, feels no such despair: "There are so many variations on the theme of life and death — the child's experience, the effect on the family; it does not lead to generalization."

These days I find myself remembering the bureau we kept in the dining room at 69 Glenmount, up against the wainscoting. It had small doors at each end, and drawers between. Here the family kept its old photos and personal letters in an untidy heap.

Our cat would satisfy his curiosity by entering one door, padding invisibly across this assortment of words and images, then emerging at the other side. "You old rascal," my father would laugh and then, perhaps, select a yellowing picture of some World War I comrade and tell what happened to him.

Much of the Creightons' past was gathered there, in disarray. I suppose the memory of this bureau comes to me now because I've tried to sort everything out.

On top of that bureau was a tattered one-volume encyclopedia brought from California, *The Circle of Knowledge*. Its "Comparative History of Nations" had columns for Egypt and Babylonia alongside one for the Hebrews: Moses lined up with Rameses III, Abraham opposite Hammurabi. This sequence went back only to 4000 BC, but over in "The Kingdoms of Nature" you saw the drawing of an ichthyosaurus swimming by a rivermouth and then, as a fossil, being covered by silt that formed just one of many layers. Evolution! The past had a shape you could figure out.

So, what pattern does the last century present, in *Empress* terms? Starting with a world divided into European empires, it ended with US-style imperialism. Canadians grew out of one colonial outlook only to receive another. Our southern neighbour's outpourings flow onto the screen, too many to be unscrambled.

Since childhood I have wanted to unscramble everything from Ichthyosaurus to Abraham, then all the way down to myself and whatever might lie ahead. With world mythology as the key. Raw experience is one thing and truth-seeking quite another, for me vastly more exciting.

But such inquiry was bound to disturb my father's worldview. East Toronto corps gave him direct experience of our humanity in all its turmoil, the Bible sufficing to lend perspective — much as market fundamentals now suffice to rule the media's vision of life.

How would Will's generation have received my free-thinking survey of these past events? The bare facts might have pleased it better. And yet if you put all the facts together, they will still not easily *lead to generalization.*

Alice Munro's *Lives of Girls and Women* gives a daunting image: Uncle Craig's history of Wawanash County — "more pages than *Gone with the Wind*," "He typed it so beautifully, no mistakes" — left in the cellar and turned by flood waters into "just a big wad of soaking paper." Young Del Jordan, Munro's *alter ego*, goes on to write her own account in the hope that every detail will become "radiant, everlasting."

Yet no matter how you try to tell it there will be enigma, mystery, the inexpressible. Munro once told humbly how a story comes to her: "I sit in a corner of the chesterfield and stare at the wall, and I keep getting it, and *getting* it, and when I've got it enough in my mind, I start to write. And then, of course, I don't really have it at all."

THE FARM

ON A HILL SOUTH of Bolton, Ontario, I visit the cemetery where Gordon and Edith Dennis now rest. In their wedding photo, his Royal Flying Corps pin is at her throat. When she died in 1988, the last *Empress* orphan, it was buried along with her.

Gordon's strong Methodist background once made him refuse to attend a function that included a turn on the dance-floor. Edith adamantly attended, however, and on her return was asked anxiously by him, "Did you dance?" To his relief she said no.

On Edith's ninetieth birthday, after his passing, a gala party was held for her. Her daughter, Bertha, once showed me the commemorative book, which holds an amazing photo. Beholding this image, I did a double-take and asked, "This isn't Aunt Edie dancing, is it?"

"Yes," she replied. "That was only the second time she had ever done it."

Edith Creighton
and
Gordon Dennis,
circa 1919.

I drive over to what is now Centreville Creek Road, where the Dennis farm is still cultivated. On our trips up from Toronto, suspense would rise over who would be the first to spot this hundred-acre paradise.

Venturing past the all-important animal-containing gate, I walk down the long driveway to the farmhouse, long unoccupied and ravaged by vandalism. A wash of sunset red plays on its stone surface, the background in many group photos.

In front downstairs was the parlour, closed off for decades with no explanation given. The mysterious Other Room, for Edith alone. Here the apple of her father's eye, "Tootsie," endured that annual late-May collapse. During childhood I sensed in Edith a mystery not evident in my other relatives.

"Her nerves have been giving her considerable trouble," Will wrote as middle age advanced, "and she has been unable to stand the excitement of visitors during this time." Edith grieved for her parents and then for Cyrus, to whom she had been a second mother. There might have been more than sorrow over the *Empress*: anger as well, perhaps.

"I am sure it will turn out all right though we did shed some tears," said Bertha in her last letter. "It is hard to leave you behind but will be for the good of all concerned." But had it really been necessary for both parents to go? There is a question about this, a question about independence and risk and encounter.

In 1923 both Arthur and Cyrus came here for a family reunion — the first since bereavement, and destined to be the last. Taken then was the orphans' only group picture in maturity: seated, Cyrus, Will and Arthur; standing, Edith and Gordon, Wilfred and Violet.

Empress orphans in maturity, with spouses, 1923.

"I cannot help feeling how changed everything is since Cyrus has gone," Wilfred later wrote to Will. "But if we all live in readiness the few years which separate us will seem as nothing when we have all passed to the beyond." Letters went back and forth between the brothers, trying to find how to pay those medical and funeral bills.

The orchard's very identity is lost, as forest reclaims the land. I am startled by a nearby sound: only the garage's side door, blown by the wind.

The barn is junk-filled, but stalls once occupied by the cows and a terrifying bull remain. Memory supplies the drumming of milk into cans, a drone of flies, cats lapping at saucers, the feel of hot eggs collected in the hen coop, the pigpen's squalor (homilies of the Prodigal Son), the excitement of leaping in the hay mow with my cousins.

Alternatives to factory toil, as shown by Booth's *In Darkest England*, would have been modest family farms such as this. Before the twentieth century rendered them obsolete, Gordon made the dream a reality. He avoided change, preferring horses to tractors — turning away from the machine, perhaps, after traumas of warfare.

Creighton males earnestly clung to pastoral values belonging to this older way of life. Having seen farming up close in Sussex, they exulted in the Dennises' return to the land. "I enjoyed reading of your naming all the animals," my father wrote to Edith as her farm life began. "Just think of the time Noah would have needed if he had named all his animals."

That is sentiment, the truth being quite a different matter.

The threat of accident was ever present. A tractor once threw Gordon off, and the wheel went over his chest. A pitchfork fell off the wagon, the handle down, and a tine went through his arm. He would treat these things as if nothing had happened.

Gordon's son Joe, who still farms up at Harriston, would have nothing to do with cattle. "I'd seen quite a bit of dairy farming working with Dad," he told me, "and I didn't want to get tied up with it seven days a week."

Today, the number of full-time farmers in Canada sinks well below 100,000. Most run high-efficiency operations quite unlike the those at Gordon's farm, now used primarily as a source of hay. The land is designated as agricultural, but only until someone pulls enough strings to have it rezoned.

Still extant is the milkhouse where Gordon would quietly sample the product of his labour. All the cousins knew that when a bullet was extracted, horsehairs from the uniform remained in the wound to cause severe infection until their removal in a second operation.

Here I would sit with my uncle, keen to know what happened to him but unable to ask. His two-engine-biplane bomber type was only then being superceded. Now Gordon, so recently at technology's frontier, contented himself with a farmer's life.

The Concorde jet crashing last week was equipped with engines developed for British nuclear bombers of the 1950s. *Titanic*-style news proliferated — "Jet-set drawn to its glamour," "Europe's grand project sped into the sunset" — amid horror that this machine's soul so fatally lost its function.

The problem with Gordon's DH-9, weak engines, gave ample time for enemy pilots to draw a bead. His attack force's mission in northern France was to bomb the foe into collapse, yet this goal became ludicrous.

After Gordon's death I was given a chance to read his wartime diary. At first he took practice flights — not yet having become part of a "show" — and one entry shows his emphasis shifting from quest to survival:

> 30 AUG *The squadron set out in the morning on a raid. It was a thrilling sight to see them take off, & felt a longing to be with them. . . Warnick was the first one to land on the drome, & as I watched him taxi in I noticed that no observer was visible & I realized what it meant (He had been shot thru the neck) I shall never forget the feeling I had when I realized this.*

Even aloft, warriors were only cogs within the larger mechanism. And death in the skies held a special horror beyond what was endured on earth.

Gordon's unit aimed to cut the main German railway into northeastern France, and force a general retreat. Navigation depended solely on map reading, and the observers often became muddled when clouds were thick.

> 13 SEP *All got lost in the clouds*
> 14 SEP *Called early in morning & went in show to Metz.*

*Encountered lots of Huns & got wounded. Got back OK & went
to Hospital.*
15 SEP Condition serious
16 SEP Hospital. Still serious
19 SEP Much better
20 SEP Out of danger

Gordon Dennis, with a medal and a wound. The result of one machine doing violence to another, up in the air: a metaphor for the *Storstad* and the *Empress*.

I go down to the Creek, a tributary of the Humber, that flows behind the farm. This stream was among the farm's greatest wonders the year round, being used both for skinny dips (significant for the study of gender differences), and boisterous hockey games.

Still plentiful here are flat rocks such as the clan would assemble into leaky dams. There was a disused road and its crumbling bridge, seen on each visit to have collapsed a bit more. For me this suggested the weight of time that drained vitality, year by year, from my aunt and her war-hero husband.

In 1936 with my father's return to Canada, all four of the surviving orphans were reunited at last. Someone shot movie footage from the creek bed of the ravine edge above, as all of us walked toward it and thus into camera view — quite a shot, suggesting the thrill of togetherness at the old farm.

We also gathered for a sublime photo that shows each family defined, fortuitously, by tent ropes and a prominent gable.

Arthur and Alma posed at one side with their firstborn, John, and baby Robert. Beside them, against a corner of the tent, were Gordon and Edith with little Bertha and Joe in his good suit. A patch of sky delimited the space where Doris stood with me, and Will with Fred. The very picture of joy was Wilfred, embracing young Gord and Art while Vi held Win; their eldest, Bill, probably clicked the shutter.

An image of harmony, love, relief after storm.

Tall weeds obstruct my path to the farmhouse. Vandals long ago broke the windows, tore off the doors, hauled away the antique stove and its fixtures. The place brings me to tears, as always. Like the *Empress*, something once magnificent has been deeply corroded by time.

Empress orphans with families, 1936.

I climb to bedrooms that were often bitterly cold, even in summer. Here at night, falling asleep, Joe and I would talk about a movie called *Captains of the Clouds* which, with only a few mushy parts, told how a Canadian bush pilot joined up and fought valorously in the air. That was our dream.

Edith continued to live in this home after Gordon's passing, long into old age. Her granddaughters found it exciting to stay with her overnight. "Leaving at night, we'd see Grandma standing at the gate, waving and waving all the time until we got to the end of that lane," recalled Glenna Holtby, the youngest. "I felt badly leaving her all alone, even though she was totally self-sufficient."

The oldest, Lynne Van Beek, at Christmas in 1997 received from her mother a lovely set of tortoise-shell combs, "the gift of the Magi." These had been given to Bertha Creighton in 1912, by a friend who would drown with her two years later.

To *The Globe and Mail* Lynne contributed a moving article about the *Empress* disaster, telling of a human cost that still has to be paid. The book she plans to write will be a revelation of Edith's world: that dark place you must not enter.

In the kitchen, mentally I put back what ought to be there. Piled-up copies of the *Globe* (full baseball box-scores). A big glass cylinder of oil for the stove. A radio that started as soon as it was turned on, being battery-operated. Beehive Corn Syrup cans with labels exchangable for glossy photos of NHL stars.

This is where we all gathered, at a table lit by the lamp with fiery little bags that never burnt. Here the adult Creightons championed or condemned Franklin Delano Roosevelt and William Lyon Mackenzie King. Vehemently they would argue for and against governmental aid, not guessing how pervasive it would soon become — and lessening the kind of anguish felt at the numbing cost of Cyrus's illness and interment.

So tiny the room now appears. Its gaping window gives a view, all along the horizon, of lights heralding the city's advance. Hard to believe how we once sat here, united by bonds of kinship and faith.

The final rural gathering was in 1968, at a nearby farm Joe had recently bought. Here the *Empress* orphans posed for what turned out to be their last group photo.

The farm's true spirit is contained in a snapshot taken during

1929, a few months before the Great Depression began. Between the barn and a stone wall, the three brothers stand exultantly with Gordon. The life of the soil: hard work lightened by good humour. Like Stephen Leacock up in Orillia, like Grandfather William at Creightonville, they wanted to be country squires in places small enough for people to know one another by name.

Gordon Dennis with Arthur, Will, Wilfred, 1929.

"You say that he went out and picked a basket of pears from the top of the tree, which is indeed strange," Will wrote to Edith, "but when you come to say that Gordon has just brought in the eggs and some milk from the cow, it is rather hard to believe, and if this cow is called Modest, goodness knows the fabulous possibilities of a cow whose abilities would warrant another name."

Here is the kind of talk our clan liked to indulge in. Laboured jokes, puns, wry anecdotes, ironic observations, wisecracks, howlers: togetherness bred such homemade verbal efforts.

I stand by the lane where we made many farewells, everyone trying for a witty last remark. Then, homeward drives in the farm-country night inspired dread as I thought of rising early to resume endless "chores" beneath skies that could suddenly turn cruel: this was the reality, the truth, of human life. And each farm seen through the car windows appeared so isolated, so vulnerable, beneath the brilliant stars.

ACKNOWLEDGEMENTS

To make acknowledgement, in Army terms, is to count your blessings. And what a gift David and Bertha Creighton gave to their descendants: the Blood of surrender, the Fire of aspiration. A blessing also for me to have known their offspring: Wilfred, the anchor; Edith, the feminine bond; Will, the soldier who returned; Arthur, who carried David's task forward.

I am fortunate to have had this book's aims realized at Dundurn Press: by my editor, Barry Jowett; by its designer, Jennifer Scott; by an editorial co-ordinator any publishing house would be lucky to have, the wondrously cordial Tony Hawke.

Karl Larson and Barbara Bawks, at the George Railton Heritage Centre, gave enormous help in the true Army spirit. I cherish the companionship found with David and Beverly Ivany of Montreal; with Yvon Vannin and Réal Gagnon of Rimouski; and Louis Bolduc of Quebec City.

For the utmost in precision about Empress details I owe a great deal to David Saint-Pierre, formerly of the Musée de la Mer in Rimouski. Stimulating insights were lent by David Zeni, author of Forgotten Empress; and by Heather Friedle of the Mariner's Museum in Newport News.

I am deeply grateful to Mark Reynolds — for Empress specifics, for strong support, for involving me in the Lost Liners project — and to other divers, notably Philippe Beaudry and Stephen Brooks. Ed and Barbara Kamuda of the Titanic Historical Society made key contributions to my awareness; I also thank Mark Rudd and Michel Villeneuve for arranging my visit with THS friends in Rimouski. Jim McFall offered similar help at Kvaerner, in Govan.

Perspectives lent by Dr. Robert Ballard took me into a new dimension; my warmest gratitude extends to "Mr. Chomping-at-the-bit" and to his gracious wife, Barbara Earle Ballard. Partisan Pictures gave my efforts an exceptional boost: Peter Schnall, of course, by his on-camera questioning; and Hannah Koltuv by her charm and enthusiasm.

Over a lengthy span of time I have gained creative incentive from four exceptional ex-students: Greg Gatenby, Mark Summers, Marni Jackson, Mike Cartmell.

Violet Creighton is always a source of inspiration. So are my cousins — Bob, Barb, and Pat, Art and Win and Betty and Bill, Birdie and Joe — and, in the next generation, Paul Creighton and Lynne van Beek. A major spur to my endeavour was Lynne's Globe article, and the concerns we later shared. Patricia Phenix's friendship has been stimulating.

The book could not have been conceived without my brother Fred's help: I relied on his clarifications of Salvationist matters, the reams of photocopied material he provided, the heartfelt encouragement he gave to someone who followed a different path.

What to include in this book, and what to leave out? Reading much of the MS to my wife Judy, I could readily sense which was which. Altogether aside from her expertise with language, she has given help not adequately to be conveyed in words.

"Open the Door, open the Door, they are waiting for me," was Gilbert's sweet command in delirium. Who were waiting for him, all we possess we would give to know — Anguish at last opened it, and he ran to the little Grave at his Grandparents' feet — All this and more, though is there more? More than Love and Death? Then tell me its name!

Emily Dickinson, Letter 873 (upon the death of her beloved eight-year-old nephew; to Mrs. J G Holland, 1883)